Biblical Money Management

The Rev. Dr. W. Maynard Pittendreigh

BIBLICAL MONEY MANAGEMENT

Copyright © 2024 by Dr. W. Maynard Pittendreigh
All rights reserved.
No part of this book may be reproduced, distributed, or transmitted in any form or by any means, including photocopying, recording, or other electronic or mechanical methods, without the prior written permission of the publisher, except in the case of brief quotations embodied in critical reviews and certain other non-commercial uses permitted by copyright law. For permission requests, please contact the author at 1281 Serena Drive, Winter Park FL 32789.

All Scripture was translated from Hebrew or Greek by the author of this book.

ISBN: 9798304624350

Dedication:

To my father, Bill Pittendreigh,
and to my son, John Pittendreigh,
and to my grandson, Ryan Pittendreigh.

I am grateful that I am among four generations of men who have loved one another, gotten along together so well, and had great fun together.

May the blessings God has given us be known by others.

Table of Contents

Introduction	7
Chapter 1 - Finding Your True Wealth – It's Not Financial	11
Chapter 2 - The Most Important Financial Skill – Generosity	25
Chapter 3 - Stewardship is More than Just Charitable Giving	39
Chapter 4 - *"Danger Will Robinson!"* The Toxic Nature of Money	47
Chapter 5 - The Quicksand of Debts	51
Chapter 6 - Call 911 - I'm Already in Financial Trouble	59
Chapter 7 - To Save or Not to Save: That is NOT the Question	73
Chapter 8 - Money and Marriage	81
Chapter 9 - The Gift and Nature of Work	95
Chapter 10 - A Hard Financial Skill to Learn: Patience	101
Chapter 11 - Good at Any Age – Thrifty Living	109
Chapter 12 - Finding Contentment and Peace With What You Have	115
Chapter 13 - Homework! Listening to the Secular Counsel	123

Introduction

Let me begin by sharing two things I have never told anyone before writing this book.

First, I have failed my parishioners. As a pastor with over 40 years of service, I have watched my parishioners suffer from financial problems while my wife and I seemed to enjoy blessings. But who was I to give financial advice? I am not a financial manager. I had no special qualifications in personal financials.

However, I have four degrees in biblical studies and theology. I should have realized earlier that while I have no special background in financial management, I have a depth of biblical knowledge. No, the Bible is not a book about financial management, but it does offer wisdom that can influence one's personal finances. That source of wisdom has, even without a financial background, given me guidance to enjoy the blessings of security.

The second secret I have not shared is how well I have done financially. As I say, I am a pastor. My first church paid me less than any of my colleagues in my seminary class. Several times my church treasurer would call me and apologetically tell me that there were not enough funds to pay me my salary for that month. "Pay what you can," I would say, "and we'll worry about the rest later."

The last church I served before retirement never gave me an increase, as they believed strongly that pastors should never receive a raise. My wife? She was a public-school teacher. You may not know what a schoolteacher makes, but you probably have an understanding that it is not much. And yet, having low to modest income in our two jobs, we entered retirement with a net worth that defined us as wealthy. Yet, I was very private about my finances. I failed my parishioners in that I could have said, "Look, this is how much I have in savings and investments – what I have done can work for others, and maybe it can work for you."

Kiplinger, the magazine on personal finance, published an article by Neale Godfrey, which posed the question of how being wealthy was defined in America. She wrote in 2024, "It takes an average net worth of $2.5 million to qualify a person as being wealthy, a bit of an uptick from $2.2 million in the surveys from 2022 and 2023. (Net worth is the sum of your assets minus your liabilities.)"

I was in that category. Granted, I was not too far into the wealthy category, but I was there. My sense of privacy almost always prevented me from sharing this with parishioners. When I did try to give some biblical financial advice, parishioners often responded with a comment that I was not qualified to give such counsel. After all, what did I know about money management. I was a pastor married to a public-school teacher, and with a salary that was public, I was usually making less than most of my parishioners. But I knew that secret – biblical principles had put me in a much better financial condition than most of my parishioners.

I didn't win a lottery, primarily because in order to win, you have to actually buy tickets. I never inherited a large sum of money. I never found a hidden treasure.

But after my wife and I married, one of our first decisions as husband and wife was to govern our actions involving money by biblical principles. It is true that I don't have the qualifications to be a financial advisor, but I have had some success in handling money based on biblical principles. When it comes to understanding and applying biblical principles, I do have a Bachelor of Arts in Bible and Religion, a Master of Divinity, a Master in Church Business Administration, and a Doctor of Ministry.

Many years ago, I bought a book that guided me on how to buy insurance, how to buy a home, how to negotiate a price for a car, and how to evaluate and invest in stocks. That book helped me as a young man, but the book you are holding is NOT that book. I am, as I've said, not a financial manager. I am a biblical scholar and with that credential, the book you are holding in your hand is all about the wisdom the Bible offers. This book may not lead you to great financial wealth, but it does offer you a way of finding security and peace with finances that the world cannot offer.

Chapter 1
Finding Your True Wealth – It's Not Financial

Much of what I have learned about managing my money has come from my parishioners. Sometimes this has come from an older church member giving me advice. Most of the time, it has come from me observing a church member make a terrible mistake. They might get themselves deep in debt, or they lose everything through gambling, or they have a mindset that simply cannot conceive of saving or thrift.

Most of the time it is a failure to invest in the right things. I'm not discussing investing in Apple or Amazon at the right time. I'm talking about the things that are of real value.

I had the opportunity to talk to an old college buddy once. We talked about our families. Like me and a lot of our classmates, he had married at or shortly after our college graduation. He and his wife had a child, then came the divorce, and 25 years later he was lamenting his loneliness.

"I've been selfish," he told me. "I never invested my time in anyone other than myself. I'm all alone. I have a daughter I barely know and a grandchild I've never met."

A parishioner shared this story of his family. He had several nephews and nieces. When his father, their grandfather or great-grandfather, died he gathered some of them and reminded them that it had been his Dad who often gathered us together for meals, holidays, and celebrations. "We need to think through this and be more intentional about staying in touch. We are spread out over several states, and if we don't think this through, we'll lose those wonderful times together."

Out of that conversation, my church member planned a family reunion, but one nephew and niece did not attend. It was a cruise to the Bahamas. The church member knew money might be an issue. As the organizers, the travel agent gave him free trip. That is a common practice in the travel business. He offered his free ticket to my nephew, who declined it.

"Family is just not that important to me," he said.

That saddened my parishioner, but it was his nephew's choice. No one was going to force him to join in a family reunion cruise, or to get together for a Thanksgiving meal.

Fast forward a decade or two, and the nephew was losing touch with his sons and was not experiencing the relationship with his grandson that he had with his own grandfather.

"I should have invested time with family," he told me.

This is the first principle of biblical money management. Money is not the one true treasure in life. There are many other things of importance. You must discover, guard, nurture, and invest in your greatest treasure.

Jesus said in Matthew 6:19-21, *"Do not store up for yourselves treasures on earth, which moths and pests destroy, and for which thieves can break in and steal. Store up treasures for yourselves in heaven, where moths and pests do not steal, and thieves cannot break in and steal.* **Where your treasure is, there is where your heart will be.***"*

Zig Zeigler was a motivational speaker and said many times, "Money can buy a house, but it can't buy a home." Money is limited. It will not provide happiness, but it will provide you with food. housing and physical security. You need money for many things that you need for living.

But don't let money be the most important driving force and goal in your life. While you are investing in stocks and bonds, invest in your family. Give time to volunteer to serve others. Build relationships with others. Be there for your friends, and they will be there for you.

Money can do a lot of good things in our life, but it is just a tool, not the goal. In the end, it cannot save us.

Not long ago I read an article in the newspaper about a hospital in a Midwestern city where officials discovered that the firefighting equipment had never been connected. For 35 years it had been relied upon for the safety of the patients in case of emergency. But it had never been attached to the city's water main. The pipe that led from the building extended 4 feet underground -- and there it stopped! The medical staff and the patients felt complete confidence in the system. They thought that if a blaze broke out, they could depend on a nearby hose to extinguish it. But theirs was a false security. Although the costly equipment with its polished valves and well-placed outlets was adequate for the building, it lacked the most important thing -- a source of water!

And that is the way it is with many of us. We trust in something that looks like it can do the job, but it is absolutely useless. Money has no power to give us happiness, and yet, we trust in it all too easily.

The best book of the Bible about money is Ecclesiastes. As a pastor, I have found that many of my generation know of the Book of Ecclesiastes as a song by the Byrds. My son's generation would respond, "The who?" And to that, I would reply, "Not the Who, they sang Tommy. The Byrds. They recorded it in 1965, and it became a hit record." Of course, my oldest sister would have known it was a song written by Pete Seeger in 1959. But well-versed readers of the Bible of any generation would know those lyrics were much older than the 20th Century. They had been written by Solomon, who lived around 3,000 years ago.

To everything there is a season,
and a time to every purpose under the heaven:
A time to be born, and a time to die;
a time to plant, and a time to pluck up that which is planted;
A time to kill, and a time to heal;

a time to break down, and a time to build up;
a time to weep, and a time to laugh;
a time to mourn, and a time to dance;
a time to cast away stones, and a time to gather stones together;
a time to embrace, and a time to refrain from embracing;
a time to get, and a time to lose;
a time to keep, and a time to cast away;
a time to tear apart, and a time to sew;
a time to keep silence, and a time to speak;
a time to love, and a time to hate;
a time of war, and a time of peace.

When I read Ecclesiastes, I picture Solomon as an old man. Really old. I picture him confined in bed with tubes up his nose kind of old. I imagine an ancient Sean Connery or Patrick Stewart. I read these words hearing the voice of an old man at the end of his life. He has made mistakes and enjoyed success, and now we sit at his death bed and hear wisdom.

In Ecclesiastes 2:10-11, this ancient man speaks: *"I denied myself nothing my eyes desired; I refused my heart no pleasure. My heart took delight in all my labor, and this was the reward for all my toil. Yet when I surveyed all that my hands had done and what I had worked hard to achieve, everything was meaningless, a chasing after the wind; nothing was gained under the sun."*

Or to put it succinctly: wealth **cannot provide lasting satisfaction.** Imagine one of the famous billionaires of our day being close to death and saying those words: "All I had done and what I worked to achieve is meaningless, a chasing after the wind."

Money is a great tool, but it is not the goal. The goal is to provide for yourself and your family. The goal is to have and to be a good friend to one's neighbor. The goal is to help the community and to respond to those in need. Money is a tool, but it is not the goal. Yes – I know I am being repetitious here, but for two reasons. First, I'm a preacher and preachers love to repeat stuff in sermons! Second, we learn through hearing and reading something over and over! And to prove I am a preacher who believes we learn through repetition, let me add this: Money is a great tool, but it is not the goal.

Jim Carrey is a well-known actor and comedian. He has been very open about his experiences with the pitfalls of fame and wealth. He once said, "I think everybody should get rich and famous and do everything they ever dreamed of so they can see that it's not the answer."

John D. Rockefeller was the world's first billionaire and one of the wealthiest men in history. In the last part of his life, he was plagued by health issues and a feeling of dissatisfaction, he recognized that his money hadn't brought him peace. In his 50s, he suffered from stress-related ailments, leading him to drastically change his priorities. He spent the rest of his life focused on philanthropy, creating the Rockefeller Foundation and funding numerous educational, public health, and scientific initiatives. This shift highlighted his realization that giving back was far more fulfilling than accumulating more wealth.

Jean-Paul Getty never seemed to have learned the lesson. He was one of the richest men of his time and had great success in business, but not in happiness.

His 16-year-old grandson was kidnapped in 1973 and Getty had to deal with the demand of a $17 million ransom demand. Getty initially refused to pay, suspecting it could be a ploy and expressing concerns about setting a precedent for other ransom demands. Even after receiving a gruesome piece of his grandson's ear as proof of the kidnappers' intentions, Getty continued to negotiate, ultimately paying only $2.2 million – the maximum amount he could claim as a tax deduction! As one might expect, this strained his relationship with family and the world. Getty was married and divorced five times and his relationships with his children and grandchildren became distant and strained. By the time of his death in 1976, Getty's fortune was estimated to be around $6 billion, yet he lived his last years in relative isolation, surrounded by wealth but largely estranged from his family.

Or as Solomon would have said, "All I had done and what I worked to achieve is meaningless, a chasing after the wind." And yes, that is another repetition, but it's worth reading again!

On the other hand, there is Warren Buffett. Although one of the richest people in the world, Warren Buffett has often spoken about the limits of wealth in providing happiness. He lives modestly, still residing in the same house he bought in 1958. He often shares that material possessions do not bring joy. Buffett has said, "The happiest people do not necessarily have the best of everything; they just make the best of everything." His philosophy centers on valuing relationships, humility, and generosity, exemplified by his significant charitable contributions and commitment to giving away the majority of his wealth.

One of the reasons wealth cannot satisfy is that it can be temporary and uncertain. Turning again to Ecclesiastes, the writer said, *"Whoever loves money never has enough; whoever loves wealth is never satisfied with their income. This, also, is meaningless."* (5:10).

We need money in our society. Unless you are an isolated farmer living off the grid, you need money for food, shelter, health care, and so many things that make life bearable, possible, and enjoyable. But it is addictive, and we often find ourselves falling into the temptation of Greed.

Jesus said in Luke 12:15, *"Watch out! Be on your guard against all kinds of greed; life does not consist in an abundance of possessions."*

Sam Polk wrote an amazing piece in the New York Times on January 18, 2014. The article was titled "For the Love of Money."

He started his article by saying this: "In my last year on Wall Street my bonus was $3.6 million — and I was angry because it wasn't big enough. I was 30 years old, had no children to raise, no debts to pay, no philanthropic goal in mind. I wanted more money for exactly the same reason an alcoholic needs another drink: I was addicted."

The article is quite long and detailed and describes how he became addicted to greed. Toward the end, he wrote this: "Dozens of different types of 12-step support groups — including Clutterers Anonymous and On-Line Gamers Anonymous — exist to help addicts of various types, yet there is no Wealth Addicts Anonymous."

One might add, there is no Greed Anonymous. Why not? Sam Polk answered in his article: "Because our culture supports and even lauds the addiction."

There is a story about a young New York investor who was vacationing in a small coastal Mexican village. He stood looking out into the cool Gulf waters. Near him was a tanned, weathered fisherman bringing onto the pier a large catch of fish.

He asked the man how long it took to catch this many fish.

"Not long at all," the fisherman replied.

"Well, why not stay out longer and catch more fish?" the young New Yorker asked smiling.

"I have enough for today," said the fisherman, "this is what I need to feed my family."

"What do you do with the rest of your time?" the young man asked curiously.

"I sleep late, fish a little, play with my children, take a siesta with my wife, Maria, and stroll into the village each evening where I enjoy some wine and laughter with friends. It's a full and happy life," the fisherman replied.

"Well, I'm a Harvard MBA and I think I can help you. You could spend more time fishing and with the proceeds from the larger catch, buy a bigger boat. Then you could catch even more fish. With those profits, you could buy several more boats and hire captains to fish for you, and eventually, you could open your own cannery. Then you would control the product, processing, and distribution. You would need to leave this small coastal village and move to Mexico City or LA or even New York where you could run your expanding enterprise."

"How long would that all take?" asked the somewhat bewildered fisherman.

"Fifteen, maybe twenty years, max."

"But then what?"

"Well, when the time was right, you could sell your company stock to the public and become very rich. You could be worth millions," declared the proud young investor.

"Millions? Wow! Then what?"

"Then you could retire and move to a small coastal village like this one where you could sleep late, fish a little in the morning, play with your grandkids, take a siesta, and enjoy wine and music with your friends in the evening."

The fisherman looked at him and asked, "Isn't that what I'm doing right now?"

There is a similar story that is attributed to a conversation between authors Kurt Vonnegut and Joseph Heller. In this anecdote, Vonnegut tells Heller that their billionaire host at a party has made more money in a single day than Heller ever did from his successful novel "Catch-22."

Heller responds, "Yes, but I have something he will never have... enough." Or as the writer of Ecclesiastes 5:10, reminds us, *"Whoever loves money never has enough; whoever loves wealth is never satisfied with their income."*

Remember what Paul said in his New Testament Letter to the Philippians? *"I have learned to be content whatever the circumstances. I know what it is to be in need, and I know what it is to have plenty. I have learned the secret of being content in any and every situation, whether well fed or hungry, whether living in plenty or in want."* (Philippians 4:11-12)

This brings us back to Ecclesiastes, which in 4:6 says, *"Better is a hand full of contentment than two handfuls of work that is a 'chasing after the wind.'"*

What brings you that tranquil contentment in life? Where is your true and cherished treasure?

This is where biblical financial planning begins. You learn to be content in all situations. You must learn where your real treasures are.

Is it having the best or most expensive car? Is it the square footage of your home? Is it your tailored suit, brand name purse, or your net worth?

Or is it in your family? Your friendships? Is your treasure having the time and resources to help your neighbors when they need help, or to offer comfort to a stranger you will never see again?

I became a pastor long ago and lived most of my life in ministry. The pay was often low, and it was never great. I worked long hours and often was often called in on my day off. It was stressful and demanding.

But I accepted the long hours in favor of flexible hours. I never missed my son's basketball or soccer games. I made a positive difference in the lives of my parishioners and in the community. I won't pretend to say that I enjoyed being with people as they died, but I will say it was an honor and deeply meaningful to me to be with them. I won't lie and say I enjoyed every committee meeting or fundraising event, but I really loved preaching, teaching, and working with the poor and the lonely.

And in the end, when I came to retirement, I found that I was blessed in financial ways, as well as in love, family, and friends. I had more money than I ever expected to have, but the money was not my treasure. It was a tool. And my security was not in my bank and investments, but in God.

Again, I ask, what is your treasure?

When you can answer that, you are ready to turn the page and learn the other principles of biblical money management.

Questions for Thought

1. What are your treasures? Make a list of five to ten treasures. Let me give you permission to include material things as well. You might name your house or your investments. Grandmother's wedding ring might be on the list. For me I would include my Great Grandfather's handwritten diary covering over 40 years. I would include one of my telescopes, a Questar that my father bought me for Christmas in 1968.

2. As for yourself, what is it that makes these material possession so important. It may well be that they represent other treasures that are dearer. My telescope can easily be replaced, but it represents a very true treasure, which is the relationship I had with my Dad.

3. Where does your family fit into this list?

4. What about God, where is the Lord in this list?

5. Where does money fit into this list?

Chapter 2
The Most Important Financial Skill - Generosity

My wife and I got married on August 23, 1975. She had just graduated from college and was working in a fast-food restaurant. She was working below the legal minimum wage, which meant she was also looking for a better job. I had two classes left – Hebrew and Art, the hardest and easiest classes I would ever take. I was working half-shift as a "lint head" in a textile mill. Together we made $345.97. We had $545.78 in savings, mostly from what I had earned in part-time jobs and small wedding gifts. Our expenses totaled $173.66. I kept a record of everything, and still have the ledger book.

Three months later, Ginny had found a new job. I was then working as a manager of a quaint little Italian restaurant - Pizza Hut. Our expenses had increased to $322.55, but our income had also increased to $1,155.82. Our savings had increased to over $1,000.

But we were not giving anything to our church or any other charity. It was my wife who pointed this out and insisted that we begin to tithe.

In my upbringing, our churches talked about "offerings" or "pledges." In hers, it was the biblical term, "tithe." Her approach was to give the first fruits. Mine was to give what's left over and to put that in the offering plate.

I have to admit, my wife was biblically correct.

The word "tithe" comes from the Old English *teogothian,* meaning "tenth." In Hebrew the word is מַעֲשֵׂר, or "maaser." This word refers to a tenth part of one's produce or earnings, which is set aside as an offering to God. In the Old Testament, it is primarily used to describe the practice of giving a tenth of one's agricultural produce or livestock to support the Levitical priesthood and the work of the temple.

So, my wife said we had to tithe, and I had to agree.

A tithe is a discipline. It is like paying the rent or mortgage, or putting a certain amount into savings or retirement investments, or brushing your teeth. It is a habit, but a good habit. Once you practice it often enough, it becomes part of your life.

A tithe is also a reasonable act of sacrifice. Worship, without sacrifice, is incomplete. We don't sacrifice a cow or bird in our culture, but we do bring to God something. God has given much to us. We should give back to God and to God's people.

A tithe is proportional giving. When I was first married, my wife and I made an income of $345.97! We knew it wasn't much, but the tithe was only $34.59. We still had enough to pay for our $80 rent, our $5.20 for gasoline, and the various sums for other things. Yes, it did feel like a lot, but it was a reasonable proportion of our income.

One day, I wanted a pizza for lunch. I had just enough flour, tomatoes, spices, and mozzarella cheese. I put everything together and realized I hadn't preheated the oven. I put the pizza in and heated up the oven and waited. When I checked it, I found the edges of the pizza here a nice brown, the cheese was perfectly melted, but right smack in the middle was a surprise.

You see, the $80 dollars we paid for rent was low, even in 1975. The place was falling apart, the front door was really just leaning in place, the landlord never cut the grass so that we had to wade through a grass jungle to take clothes to the outside clothesline to dry the wash, and we were battling roaches.

There must have been a roach on the top of the oven when I turned it on. The creature died of the heat and fell right smack into the middle of my otherwise perfect pizza. One of the lessons I learned that day was to always preheat the oven!

I did the only thing I knew to do. I cut out the center of the pizza and ate the rest.

And while I ate, I thought of that tithe.

Tithing is a difficult discipline sometimes.

Leviticus 27:30 teaches us that we are to give a *"tithe of everything from the land, whether grain from the soil or fruit from the trees, belongs to the Lord; it is holy to the Lord."*

My wife and I made that commitment, and it has sometimes been a sacrifice, but what is the worship of God without some sacrifice being presented?

As a pastor, however, I never asked for people to give their tithes to the church. What I would do was to talk about developing the attitude and practice of generosity. I tried to think of my own tithe as an act of sacrifice to God and generosity to my neighbors. Most of our tithe was given to the church, but part of it went to other mission programs.

It may take a while to begin tithing. Giving 10% may be a strain that goes beyond appropriate sacrifice, so starting at 5% may be more reasonable, or even at 1%. Then each year add to that until you reach the 10% mentioned so often in the Bible.

This giving must also be joyful. Paul, in 2 Corinthians 9:6-7, wrote, *"Remember: Whoever plants little will harvest little. Whoever plants generously will harvest generously. Each of you should give what you have decided in your heart to give, not reluctantly or under compulsion, for God loves a cheerful giver."*

I remember that the church I attended as a teenager was having financial struggles. The minister would always introduce the offering with that verse, ending with "for God loves a cheerful giver," and then the ushers would walk from pew to pew passing the offering plates, into which checks and cash could be deposited.

One Sunday, after sharing with us how dire our church finances had become, he changed the verse as he introduced the offering, saying, "for God loves a cheerful giver, but he will also accept money from you grumps."

We all laughed.

But the joke got old when he did it week after week.

I learned a lesson in his attempt at humor. God loves a cheerful giver. Period. An ungrateful and ungenerous gift is tiresome and not a true and spiritual sacrifice.

This means that in learning to tithe, one must learn the discipline <u>and</u> the joy of giving.

So many times, as a pastor I have heard my church members share the joy they have received through giving. "It just makes me feel so good," I have heard.

I served the Warrenton Presbyterian Church of Abbeville, SC, early in my ministry. Every December, with the help of the Department of Social Services, we would identify a family in financial distress. One elder who worked for DSS and I would take food and toys and other gifts to the family. We would be the only ones knowing the identity of the family.

One year, we drove up to a home and I asked the elder, "Are you sure this is the place?"

It was a brand new, huge, two-storied house. It was better than my house or the home of the elder, Jimmy. We both felt we had been scammed, but we knocked on the door anyway.

A man opened the door and invited us in. There were no wallboards, just two by four frames which divided the future rooms. A woman had a child in a tub of water that was on the kitchen table, which was one of the few pieces of furniture. The water came from a well, as there was no running water. The bed was just a mattress.

The man told us his story. He was doing well at his job and started building their dream home. Then the mill cut back, and he lost his job. He finished the outside and the roof, and he was building the rest slowly, bit by bit, as money from odd jobs came in.

When we finished handing out the gifts, we said our goodbyes and got back to the car. Jimmy was sobbing. I asked him if he was okay, and he said, "these are tears of joy. I feel so good about what we've done. That could be me and my family."

Acts 20:35 has the only known quotation from Jesus that is not found in the four Gospels. Paul starts by saying, *"In all that I did, I showed you that by hard work we must help the weak. Remember the words of our Lord Jesus Christ who said, 'It is more blessed to give than to receive.'"*

At some point, you must not only learn the discipline of tithing and giving, but also the joy of generosity.

Now there is a word of warning I need to share, and that is that there is a danger in the tithe. It is found in what is often referred to as "prosperity Gospel" or by various other names: Prosperity theology, the health and wealth gospel, the gospel of success, seed-faith gospel, but by whatever name, this is a belief if you give to God, God will make you rich. It assumes God's will is for all of us to be wealthy, but that is not biblical. Some of us are called to be richer but others are called to live without great wealth.

The Washington Post published an opinion piece by Cathleen Falsani, the religion writer, which pointed to the conflict Prosperity Gospel has with traditional and basic Christian teaching. "Jesus was born poor, and he died poor. During his earthly tenure, he spoke time and again about the importance of spiritual wealth and health. When he talked about material wealth, it was usually part of a cautionary tale."[1]

So what does one do with Proverbs 3:9-10, which says, *"Honor the Lord with your wealth, with the first fruits of your crops, and THEN your barns will be filled to overflowing and your vats will be filled to the brim and over flowing with new wine."*

The Old Testament prophet, Malachi, writes in 3:8-12 of his book words often preached by the Prosperity Gospel, in which God says, "Will a mere mortal rob God? Yet you rob me." The prophet then quotes the reasonable question by the people, "How are we robbing you?"

---

[1] Falsani, Cathleen. "The Worst Idea of the Decade: The Prosperity Gospel." The Washington Post. 25 June 2015.

God replies in Malichi, *"In tithes and offerings. You are under a curse—your whole nation—because you are robbing me. Bring the whole tithe into the storehouse, that there may be food in my house. Test me in this,"* says the Lord Almighty, *"and see if I will not throw open the floodgates of heaven and pour out so many blessing that there will not be room enough to store it."*

On the surface, it seems that this means if we give to God our tithes, God MUST give wealth to us. God seems to be OBLIGATED to make us rich.

Many times, I have heard church members tell me that this works. Like the Law of Compounding Interest, or a Law of Physics, or Murphy's Law, there is this Law of Give to God and God must give to you.

No.

Let me suggest that there is something different at work here. Tithing is a discipline. It is often the first effort at budgeting many people experience. Being disciplined with money by tithing will force you to be disciplined with spending within, or even better, beneath your means.

One woman in my church shared with me, "Tithing changed everything for my family. We were in debt, we were drowning, and then we did something crazy by adding another payment – a tithe to the church. It was the first time we ever had a budget. We still eat out, but not as much. We still go on vacations, but we are much thriftier. Things started getting better. Even when I had to stop working and our income was cut in half, we seemed to be more content, more in control, and more satisfied. Abundance didn't come in more money, but more peace."

Years ago, I was doing mission work in India. My team was working mostly in schools, and on Sundays we would visit a church.

I remember visiting one church in particular. India is a nation of great wealth and deep poverty. This particular church was located in a city slum. The homes were nothing more than tents. The tents were made of moldy, rotting cloth. Everything was jammed together. There was hardly any room to walk between the tents. There was no water system and no well. People drank water that was running along the gutters of the streets.

In the midst of this slum was a little church.

It was nothing more than a concrete block building with four walls and a doorway. The roof was nothing more than some metal sheeting laid on the top of the building. The church building measured about 10 feet wide and 20 feet long, smaller than most Sunday School classes in American Churches.

Inside there were 30 people. They were all crammed together, sitting on the floor and they gave me a chair to sit in at the front of the church. If I had crossed my legs, I would have knocked out three people on the front row.

We did everything Christians do in worship.

We sang.

We prayed.

I preached with an interpreter.

And there was an offering.

I've seen poverty. I've been to third world countries. I've worked in Haiti where the poverty is universal. But here – the poverty was so deep. These were the poorest people I'd ever met.

At the time I made my visit to India, poverty in America was defined as earning $11,490 per year in a family of one. In America, 96.1% of our households living in relative poverty had a television to watch, and 83.2 percent of them had a video-recording device in case they cannot get home in time to watch the football game, or their favorite television show and they want to record it for watching later. Among America's poor, 98% had refrigerators, 93% had microwaves and 83% had air conditioning.

Do you know how they define poverty in India? I was told that the definition of poverty is to have less than a full meal per day.

And there are these people gathered in this tiny little church. When it was time for the offering, every single person gave. They gave eagerly. They reached and strained to put their single coin into the offering.

One lady had no money.

She contributed a single, tiny bag of rice.

After the service, I asked what they used the offering for. Part of it was to pay the pastor's salary, which was not much. Part of it was to buy Bibles for the church. Part of it was to go to Missions. Imagine that! Missions! They can't feed themselves, but they are giving missions to help people they will never meet. Most of it goes to feed the poor.

Feed the poor?

I thought these were the poor! I could not imagine that there would be people more impoverished than these folks!

Then I asked about the lady who gave the bag of rice.

I was told she never had any money to give. But IF she had food to eat during the day, she would carefully measure out the food and set some of it aside.

Every day – IF she had food to eat, part of it was set aside for the offering. A tenth of it. A tithe. And on Sunday, when she came to church. She would bring her bag of rice as an offering – so it could be used to feed the poor.

Imagine doing that on Monday, and Tuesday, and Wednesday, and on up to Friday. Now imagine Saturday comes and there is no food at all for yourself or the Sunday's offering. Church is tomorrow, but there on the table is the rice you've set aside every day. It would be tempting to reach into the bag and cook that rice. Skip church. Or go to church and skip the offering.

But no, she never did that. The pastor told me she always brought the bag of rice.

And here we are. The poorest among us is still among the world's richest – and yet we give begrudgingly rather than with cheerfulness, and perhaps we don't give at all.

1 Timothy 6:17 says, *"Command those who are rich in this present world not to be arrogant nor to put their hope in wealth, which is so uncertain, but rather on God who richly provides us with everything for our enjoyment. They are to do good, to be rich in good works, generous, and ready to share."*

I often find myself thinking of my time in India. Rarely do I recall the visit I made to the Taj Mahal, or the fine restaurants, or even the schools we worked in. I think of that woman. I wonder when we, here in America, will be as wealthy as that woman. When will we have enough so that we can be as generous as she?

Questions for Thought

1. When was the last time you were generous to someone you knew?

2. When was the last time you were generous to a stranger?

3. Think about how much you contribute to the church and other charities. For this, you should

spend some time and look carefully at your bank records.

4. In the same way you have looked at your giving, look at your income. What percentage of your income is given to the church?

5. What percentage of your income is given to all charities and those in need?

6. Do you believe that you should, not can, give more? If so, set a goal and consider how you might reach that goal.

Chapter 3
Stewardship is More than Just Charitable Giving

Having talked about generosity and charitable giving, we now turn to stewardship. Wait – isn't that the same thing? Not exactly.

I have my Great Aunt Helen's love seat. Great Aunt Helen died without any children, so the love seat went to her nephew, who happened to be my great grandfather, who gave it to his son, who gave it to his son – my Dad, who gave it to me. It has been in my family for 140 years.

But when my father gave it to me, I knew that it wasn't mine. It belonged to the family. I was merely the steward of this loveseat.

It now sits in my son's house, and now he is the steward of this loveseat.

To be a steward is to be responsible for something that you do not actually own. It is in your care for a time; someday it will be in someone else's care. Webster's dictionary defines stewardship as "the careful and responsible management of something entrusted to one's care."

We are all stewards in some fashion. Think about the things for which you are responsible, that are not truly your own.

Psalm 24:1 says, *"The earth is the Lord's, and everything in it, the world, and all who live in it."* In other words, it is not a short list of things like Great Aunt Lucille's loveseat, it is everything!

When I was in college, I had the opportunity to attend a worship service in which David Wilkerson was speaking. He was a courageous pastor who ministered to the violent New York gangs in the 1950s and 60s. He wrote the book, "The Cross and the Switchblade," which was made into a movie.

At the time I heard him preach, America was involved in the Apollo program. Armstrong and Aldwin had been the first to walk on the moon and we were still sending crewed missions there.

Wilkerson felt quite differently about the moon program than I did. While I was excited about it, he was angry. He said we should not go to the moon because that was God's moon!

I sat there and thought, "Isn't the earth God's earth? Where could I go that would not belong to God?"

I think about my house and all of the money I have in the bank and in investments and I'm still realizing that everything I think I have belongs to God. I'm just a steward of these things.

Stewardship is a central theme in biblical financial management. It is more than just charitable giving—it is a lifestyle of managing everything God has entrusted to us with care, purpose, and accountability. In this chapter, we will explore what biblical stewardship is, what the Bible teaches about it, and how to apply its principles in managing money and resources.

1 Corinthians 4:2 says: *"Now it is required that those who have been given a trust must prove faithful."* Stewardship is not about how much we give away but about how faithfully we manage all that we have been given.

Let's take a look at a parable that Jesus told in Matthew's Gospel. This illustrates the different ways people serve as stewards of things that are not their own.

Matthew 25:14-30
14 "It will be like a person going on a journey, who called his servants and entrusted his wealth to them. 15 To one he gave five talents, and to another one talent, each according to his ability. Then he went on his journey.

Let's stop here and let me explain that the term "talent" refers to a form of currency in the time of Jesus' ministry. It had been around for a long time, going back all the way to the time of Moses. Exodus 38:24 mentions, "All the gold that was used for the work, in all the construction of the sanctuary, the gold from the offering, was twenty-nine talents ..."

At the time of Jesus, a talent was the largest unit of currency. According to Scholars, to have a bag of five talents of gold or silver would mean being a multimillionaire by today's standards.

Let's continue with the parable Jesus tells:

¹⁶ *"The man who had received five talents went at once and put his money to work and gained five talents more. ¹⁷ So also, the one with two talents gained two more. ¹⁸ But the man who had received one talent went off, dug a hole in the ground and hid his master's money.*

¹⁹ *"After a long time the master of those servants returned and settled accounts with them. ²⁰ The man who had received five bags of gold brought the other five. 'Master,' he said, 'you entrusted me with five talents. See, I have gained five more.'*

²¹ *"His master replied, 'Well done, good and faithful servant! You have been faithful with a few things; I will put you in charge of many things. Come and share your master's happiness!'*

²² *"The man with two talents also came. 'Master,' he said, 'you entrusted me with talents; see, I have gained two more.'*

²³ *"His master replied, 'Well done, good and faithful servant! You have been faithful with a few things; I will put you in charge of many things. Come and share your master's happiness!'*

So far, so good. People are not only preserving what has been entrusted in them, they are using them for the good of the master. The master responds by saying,

"Well done, good and faithful servant!" Who would not want to hear God greet us into heaven with those words?

²⁴ "Then the man who had received one talent came. 'Master,' he said, 'I knew that you are a hard man, harvesting where you have not sown and gathering where you have not scattered seed. ²⁵ So I was afraid and went out and hid your talent in the ground. See, here is what belongs to you.'
²⁶ "His master replied, 'You wicked, lazy servant! So you knew that I harvest where I have not sown and gather where I have not scattered seed? ²⁷ Well then, you should have put my money on deposit with the bankers, so that when I returned I would have received it back with interest.
²⁸ "'So take the talent from him and give it to the one who has ten talents. ²⁹ For whoever has will be given more, and they will have an abundance. Whoever does not have, even what they have will be taken from them. ³⁰ And throw that worthless servant outside, into the darkness, where there will be weeping and gnashing of teeth.'

There are several lessons to learn from this parable:

1. **God Entrusts Us with Resources:**
   Each servant was given talents "according to his ability" (v.15). Similarly, God entrusts us with resources, opportunities, and abilities tailored to our capacity.
2. **Stewards Are Expected to Act:**
   The first two servants immediately put their talents to work and doubled their master's money (v.16-17). Stewardship involves <u>proactive</u> management and wise use of resources.

3. **Neglect Has Consequences:**
   The third servant buried his talent out of fear and was condemned as lazy and wicked (v.26). The servant claims that he knew his master was harsh and to be feared, but there is no evidence of that in the parable. On the contrary, the master entrusted a huge sum of money into their hands and rewarded the successful and faithful servants. Failing to use what God has given us for His purposes is poor stewardship.
4. **Faithfulness Is Rewarded:**
   The faithful servants were commended and entrusted with even greater responsibilities (v.21, 23). God honors faithful stewardship with greater opportunities to serve Him.

When I was in Seminary, I would preach wherever I could in order to develop my craft. Most of these were small country churches. One Sunday in 1978, in a tiny, little church, somewhere in Georgia, I stood to start the service and noticed a man jog down the center aisle. He leaned into the pulpit and said, "Don't forget to announce that today is Soil Stewardship Sunday." Before I could respond, the man was already jogging back to his pew, leaving me wondering, "what in the world is Soil Stewardship Week."

Not being a farmer, I did not know that this was a Sunday to focus people's attention on our responsibility to care for the soil and the ecology. Doing my best, I simply started the service with a vague statement, "I've been asked to announce that today is Soil Stewardship Sunday. I am sure we all know how important this is. So, with that in mind, let us stand and sing our opening hymn."

Time and again, the Bible presents the concept of stewardship. In **Psalm 24:1** we read, *"The earth is the Lord's, and everything in it, the world, and all who live in it."* Everything in the earth is God's and that includes our money. We are in the parable of the talents, and we need to remember that. As we manage our money, we should act as managers and stewards, and not as the owner.

Matthew 6:33 says, *"But seek first his kingdom and his righteousness, and all these things will be given to you as well."* As stewards, and not owners, of our money and resources, we need to align our financial decisions with God's purposes. Give generously to your church, missions, and causes that advance His kingdom.

Questions for Thought

1. Think about your money. If the whole world and all that is in it belongs to God, then so does your money. How do you feel about being the steward of God's money, rather than the owner of your own money?

2. Knowing, and acknowledging, that your money belongs to God and that you are a steward, how might you spend money differently?

Chapter 4

"Danger Will Robinson!" The Toxic Nature of Money

A few years ago, I saw some kids cutting through my yard. Once they discovered my yard was a short cut, they used it daily and were creating a pathway on the grass. I thought about allowing the grumpy old man inside me to yell at them, "Get off my lawn!" But having once been a kid myself, I knew they would still use my yard as a shortcut.

At the time, I was planting a lot of new flowers and shrubs around the yard, and it occurred to me that creative landscaping seemed to be a good solution.

Spanish Bayonet was the answer.

It is a plant with sharp points, hence the name Bayonet. It is also mildly toxic that would irritate the skin, although anyone living along the coast of Southern Georgia would know not to touch it.

After that, the kids simply went 16 feet to the side and cut through a vacant lot. Toxic plants can serve a purpose, but one does have to be careful.

Likewise, money is toxic but serves useful purposes. It should be handled with care.

I conducted the wedding for Ed and Mary, and I have watched them over the years struggle with the toxic effects of money. They never had any savings. Ed would always spend money as soon as it came into his hands. He was always in debt, and eventually became bankrupt, much to Mary's dismay. Mary, who had handled money well, eventually was infected by Ed's toxic approach to money. She had to have the best jewelry, often spending tens of thousands of dollars. Rather than a practical coat, she would buy the very expensive coat with the brand name. They would see someone take a trip or drive a certain car, and they had to have one as well. They ate at restaurants that cost top dollar.

The cost this living to impress the neighbors was Ed and Mary could not afford their medications. Ed ignored his diabetes, which eventually killed him. Mary was clinically depressed, but without her medication she became suicidal. Mary took her own life the day after Ed died. Of all those neighbors and relatives whom Mary and Ed tried to impress with their spending, only a dozen showed up at their funerals. Money and having stuff had been their goal in life, but the toxicity of money left them without love, security, and peace.

Another story is that of Jordan Belfort, a name you may not recall. You may, however, remember the movie, "The Wolf of Wall Street." Belfort, a stockbroker, is portrayed in that movie by Leonard DiCaprio. His excessive greed and unethical practices lead to his arrest. He is sentenced to prison and forced to pay restitution.

In a pivotal point of the film, actor Michael Douglas delivers a memorable line: "Greed, for lack of a better word, is good. Greed is right, greed works. Greed clarifies, cuts through, and captures the essence of the evolutionary spirit."

Jordan Belfort lost control in a world of greed and toxic money. The FBI and the courts made his life of greed a life of sorrow.

Mike Tyson was a boxing legend. He amassed a fortune of over $300 million during his career. Tyson's lifestyle included buying multiple mansions, exotic pets (like his famous tigers), luxury cars, and an extravagant wardrobe. Then in 2003, he declared bankruptcy with his debts around $23 million. Tyson has since rebuilt his life but learned hard lessons about the dangers of greed.

Paul wrote in his New Testament letter, 1 Timothy 6:10, *"The love of money is a root of all sorts of evil. Some people, eager for money, have wandered from the faith and pierced themselves with many griefs."*

This is an oft misquoted verse in the Bible, with people saying, "Money is the root of all evil," but that is not what it says. It is the "Love of money" that is evil's root.

I have said many times that money is not a goal as much as it is a tool. It helps us buy food to eat, a house to shelter us, transportation to see family, and many other good things. But it has a toxicity that may, but not necessarily, become dangerous.

Jesus, in Luke 12:15 warns us, *"Watch out! Be on your guard against all types of greed. Life does not consist in the abundance of possessions."*

Questions for Thought

1. When was the last time you experienced the toxic side of money?

2. Do you feel your money is a tool with which to do the necessary things in life, or do you feel a love for money in and of itself?

3. Have you ever regretted a donation you gave to the church, or a charity, or to an individual?

Chapter 5
The Quicksand of Debts
(Our Debts and Other People's Debts)

When I was a kid, I loved Tarzan movies, especially with Johnny Weissmuller. It seemed that every movie had Tarzan rushing to save Jane. Along the way he would have to fight the man-eating plants, the lions, snakes, the alligators, and other dangers. No danger was worse than the quicksand! As I remember it, Tarzan would fall into the quicksand and would call an elephant to come to his rescue.

As a child I lived on the edge of a forest. We all loved playing in the woods for hours, but we were always mindful of the dangerous quicksand. Everyone knew the story of little Bobby, who years earlier had died in quicksand. Sometimes we would hear how his mother watched helplessly as poor little Bobby would be pulled under and slowly disappear with only his hat floating on top.

Of course, there was never a kid in the neighborhood named "Bobby." No child had ever died in quicksand. But as kids we believed in the urban myth and knew that the woods were full of dangers!

In my 20s, I took out a loan for a car, and then a piano, and even a vacation. I felt I was becoming "little

Bobby" and that soon I would disappear into the pool of debt.

When I bought my third or fourth car, I began to reconsider debt. It seemed that as soon as I paid off one car, it was wearing out and I needed to buy another. I was always having to take out a loan because that was the way I had always bought my cars, but on one particular car purchase I took the time to consider how much loans were costing me. Buying a car for $20,000 did not mean I would pay $20,000, but closer to $23,000. Worse, I was realized that as soon as I paid off one car, it was time to buy another. By this time in my life, the interest I had paid to banks totaled over $10,000. I thought about how nice it would have been to have kept that money rather than to give it to the banks.

I decided to save for the car instead of borrowing money for the car. It took time and work, but I turned the process upside down. Instead of borrowing money and paying additional interest, I saved the money ahead of time and made the bank pay me interest.

Financial advisors would disagree. If the loan interest is 4%, but your investments earn 8% annually, financing the car leaves you financially ahead. This is absolutely true, but there was something inside me that recoiled against borrowing money.

But remember – I am not a financial advisor. I am presenting biblical principles for money management. Sometimes a loan is necessary. How could anyone buy a home without a mortgage? Emergencies come up, and we need the help that loans provide. Even avoiding car loans is impossible for the first one or more decades of adulthood. Debt is a way of life but remember "little Bobby." Even urban myths can teach us to avoid dangers.

While financial advisors can guide you into many ways to handle debts, the goal of this book is to give the reader some basic principles that come from the Bible.

Biblical principle for Debts #1: Debt Is Not Forbidden, But It Is a Burden.

Proverbs 22:7 warns us that *"The rich rule over the poor, and the borrower is servant to the lender."*

I worked in the South Carolina Department of Corrections between college and seminary. In my work as a counselor, I became aware that one of the inmates operated a loan sharking business. He had the experience, because that's why he had been arrested and thrown into our prison. For inmates, the interest rate was 25%, but for staff members, loans were interest-free. What happens when a corrections officer or even the warden owes $20,000 interest-free to an inmate? You are forced to bring in drugs and other contraband into the prison. If an inmate wanted to visit a girlfriend or go to a movie, a corrections officer provided transportation. Eventually, things caught up with these members of the prison staff and they soon joined the prison population!

Quicksand and debts, either way, it sucks you in until all that's left is your hat floating on the surface.

Brian took a more traditional loan from an actual bank. He was a construction manager but was laid off in the 2008 financial crisis. He started using credit cards to cover mortgage payments, groceries, and other necessities of life. He thought he'd find a job soon, but the debt became unmanageable. The credit card debt reached $65,000, his car was repossessed leaving him without transportation for interviews or future employment, his marriage was under great stress, and soon only his hat would be floating on top of the quicksand. He eventually filed for bankruptcy.

Brian's story is as old as time. In Nehemiah 5:1-13 we read of people who have lived through hard times, including a great famine. Israelites cried out to Nehemiah because they had to mortgage their fields, vineyards, and homes to buy food during a famine. Others borrowed money to pay taxes, which led them to sell their children into slavery.

Debt can be a great burden!

Proverbs 22:26-27 provides a cautionary warning *"Do not be one who shakes hands in pledge or puts up security for debts; if you lack the means to pay, your very bed will be snatched from under you."* This verse implies that individuals who rashly enter into debt without the means to repay lost even their most basic possessions, such as their bed, highlighting the risk of financial ruin.

Avoid debt when you can, but <u>if it is necessary, enter into it with care and caution.</u>

Biblical principle for Debts #2: Debt Must be Honored through Repayment.

Psalm 37:21 warns us, *"The wicked borrow and do not repay."* Borrowing itself is not condemned, but failure to repay is considered wicked. This suggests that debt, when managed responsibly and repaid, is not sinful, but to borrow and not repay is evil.

Biblical principle for Debts #3: Avoid Letting Debt Become Unmanageable

If you must go into debt, it is your responsibility to make sure that the debt can be managed.

I have always appreciated real estate agents I've worked with. They have helped me find wonderful homes in which to live. However, it seems to me that they always looked for the homes I could afford, but not always the ones I wanted to afford. I might be able to afford a particular home mortgage, but would I be able to afford a new car, or good clothing and food, or a nice vacation? What would happen if my income dropped? Or if the roof needed replacing?

This is one of the teachings of Romans 13:7-8 when it says *"Give to everyone what you owe them: If you owe taxes, pay taxes; if revenue, then revenue; if respect, then respect; if honor, then honor. Let no debt remain outstanding, except the continuing debt to love one another."* In his letter to the Romans, Paul acknowledges that debts can exist but advises believers to repay them promptly to avoid unnecessary burdens.

Biblical principle for Debts #4: Avoid Cosigning Loans

As I write this, I admit that I have done this once. My stepmother needed a bridge loan to move into a continuing-care retirement community (CCRC). Once there, she would have a place to live for the rest of her life. She could live in Independent Living, Assisted Living, and even Nursing Care.

With great hesitation, I co-signed her loan. To me the commandment to honor my father, who had recently died, overruled biblical wisdom to avoid being involved in someone else's debts.

It turned out well. She paid back the loan and was able to move into the CCRC of her choice. I also knew that had this turned into a worst-case scenario, I could financially manage this particular and specific situation. Still, until she paid off the loan, I had visions of "little Bobby's" hat floating on top of the quicksand.

If you ever face a similar situation, you will have to prayerfully consider what to do, but consider the Bible's counsel (not commandment, but counsel) to avoid cosigning loans.

Proverbs 22:26-27: *"Do not be one who shakes hands in pledge or puts up security for debts; if you lack the means to pay, your very bed will be snatched from under you."* This is the Bible's way of saying that cosigning can lead to financial ruin if the borrower fails to repay. It warns that you may lose your own assets if you take on someone else's debt irresponsibly.

Proverbs 17:18: *"One who has no sense shakes hands in pledge and puts up security for a neighbor."* This verse portrays cosigning as an unwise and risky decision, suggesting that it lacks prudence.

Proverbs 11:15: *"Whoever puts up security for a stranger will surely suffer, but whoever refuses to shake hands in pledge is safe."* Cosigning can lead to suffering and loss, whereas avoiding it ensures financial safety and stability.

Proverbs 6:1-5: *"My son, if you have put up security for your neighbor, if you have shaken hands in pledge for a stranger, you have been trapped by what you said, ensnared by the words of your mouth. So do this, my son, to free yourself, since you have fallen into your neighbor's hands: Go—to the point of exhaustion—and give your neighbor no rest! Allow no sleep to your eyes, no slumber to your eyelids. Free yourself, like a gazelle from the hand of the hunter, like a bird from the snare of the fowler."* This passage advises taking immediate and proactive steps to extricate oneself from a cosigning agreement, emphasizing its potential danger.

In summary:
- **Be Cautious:** Think carefully before cosigning a loan, as you could become liable for the full amount if the borrower defaults.
- **Ensure Affordability:** Only consider cosigning if you are financially able to repay the debt without jeopardizing your own stability.
- **Seek Alternatives:** If someone you care about needs help, explore other ways to assist them without putting yourself at financial risk.

- **Be Wise and Prayerful:** Seek God's guidance in financial decisions to ensure you are acting with wisdom and responsibility.

Questions for Thought

1. Have you ever felt burdened by debt? Is that a feeling you now have?

2. If you feel overwhelmed by debt, write down a plan of action for how you can get out of debt.

3. Have you ever co-signed a loan for someone? Did you think this was the right thing to do or not for those particular situations?

Chapter 6
Call 911 –
I'm Already in Financial Trouble

When I was the pastor of Chapel by the Sea on Fort Myers Beach, Florida, we operated a program for those who needed food and other assistance. It was not a universally loved program. City Hall was always trying to shut us down, fearful that any aid to the poor attracted people who might be a detriment to tourism on the island. We were often ridiculed in social media.

One day, one of my own parishioners came to me and begged me to shut it down. "When you feed the wolves, the wolves will soon take over," he told me.

I suggested that he volunteer in the program. "You might gain a different perspective when you get to know these people," I told him.

Months later, I was happy to see him at the breakfast. He was sitting with the poor and homeless, enjoying day old bagels from the local grocery store, chatting with the others at the table. In fact, I began to see him there every day.

Sadly, I learned that he was not there as a church member to volunteer, but as one who could no longer afford food. It was 2008 and the market had crashed. His pension had been cut by 75%.

All of us face the possibility of a bad economy. Many of us may face the consequences of our own bad financial decisions.

Financial trouble is a burden that can feel overwhelming, but the Bible offers hope, wisdom, and practical guidance for those facing challenges. Whether the problem is due to debt, unforeseen emergencies, or poor financial decisions, Scripture provides principles to navigate these difficulties and restore stability.

So – there you are, in financial trouble. You might soften it by referring it to "being challenged by finances," or you may be straight forward and say, "I'm up a well-known creek without a paddle."

1. Acknowledge the Situation
The first step in overcoming financial trouble is recognizing the issue and taking responsibility. The Bible teaches the importance of humility and self-awareness.

The Prodigal Son is found in Luke 15:11-32. As the story goes, the younger of two sons demands his inheritance from his father, essentially wishing him dead in cultural terms. This son leaves home, squandering his wealth in reckless and wild living. When a famine strikes, he becomes destitute and takes a degrading job feeding pigs, longing to eat the food given to the animals. Realizing his mistakes, the son decides to return home, acknowledging what he has done. He plans to ask his father for forgiveness and to be treated as a hired servant rather than a son, but the father welcomes the son and has a great feast. <u>The good result hinges on the son acknowledging his situation.</u>

Other verses offer the same advice to acknowledge the reality of your predicament. **Proverbs 28:13** says, *"Whoever conceals their failure (or sin) does not prosper, but the one who confesses and renounces them finds mercy."* To understand this verse, it helps to know that one of the Greek words for "sin" "hermartia." It means "missing the mark," as an archer might do in aiming for a target. "Failure" is another way it is translated, and "sin" is another translation.

1 John 1:9 says, *"If we confess our "hermartia"* (admitting that we have missed the financial mark), *God is faithful and just and will forgive us our sins and purify us from all unrighteousness."*

James 5:16 says, *"Therefore confess your "hermatia" to each other and pray for each other so that you may be healed. The prayer of a righteous person is powerful and effective."*

Why is it important tell others of our "hermartia?" If I miss the mark, it is not really in my nature to share it. I'm going to do everything possible to keep this a secret. But I need to understand that my pride is not helpful. Being humble brings healing.

James 4:10 says, *"Humble yourselves before the Lord, and he will lift you up."* Humility invites God's exaltation at the proper time. When we are in financial distress, whether it is our fault or that of the economy, inflation, or the layoffs at the mill, we find that when we humble ourselves and acknowledge our situation, God brings healing.

Proverbs 11:2 says, *"When pride comes, then comes disgrace, but with humility comes wisdom."* True wisdom flows from a humble heart, free of arrogance. Rod was a friend of mine who had lost his job and was debt. He came to me, and I was able to do two things. First, I helped him get a new job. Second, I introduced him to a church member who was brilliant with finances, but who, through no fault of his own, had a financial crisis that he eventually overcame. "Talk to Rex," I told Rod. "Rex has been where you are, and he has a lot of experience in these matters."

Had Rod not acknowledged his situation, he would not have gotten the job or the counsel from Rex. He had to put away his pride so that he could open himself to the help of others.

2. Seek God's Wisdom and Guidance
God cares about every aspect of your life, including your finances. When facing trouble, seek His wisdom and trust in His provision. **James 1:5** tells us: *"If any of you lacks wisdom, you should ask God, who gives generously to all without finding fault, and it will be given to you."* Pray for wisdom in making financial decisions and for God's guidance in your recovery.

3. Create a Plan for Recovery

I love Mission Impossible. I was a fan of the original television series and the newer movies. At the beginning of each mission, a voice would lay out the task before the Impossible Missions Force. Then, having laid out the challenges, the voice would say, "You mission, should you decide to accept it..."

Your mission, and I encourage you to accept it, is that if you are under financial stress, get out of it. How? The first step on Mission Impossible was to make a plan. The plans would sometimes be complex and dangerous, but always entertaining. But on television, it always worked.

In 1972, NASA sent three men in an Apollo space capsule to land on the moon. This mission, Apollo 13, was to be the third such landing on the moon. But the spacecraft encountered a crisis on the way. There was an explosion on the Service Module, which held the fuel and oxygen and the engines for providing them with thrust to the moon and home again.

This was worse than any financial crisis. Lives were at stake.

Before they did anything else, they made a plan. The first steps had to be done immediately. They had to stabilize power usage, conserve oxygen and water, and figure out how to navigate back to Earth without the primary systems.

Their main decision was whether to turn around and come back to earth, which sounded like the best decision. But careful planning helped NASA realize that it would take more power and fuel, so they continued onto the Moon and then returned without landing on the Moon.

Along the way, other problems developed, but each time they addressed the issue calmly and formulated a plan. Apollo 13 came home. It was described as a "successful failure."

The Bible emphasizes the importance of planning and diligence, especially in times of crisis.

Proverbs 21:5 says, *"The plans of the diligent lead to profit as surely as haste leads to poverty."* A well-thought-out plan is essential for your financial recovery.

This plan might include some of the following:

- A realistic budget that prioritizes necessities like housing, food, and utilities.
- Listing your debts and developing a repayment plan, focusing on high-interest loans first.
- Cutting unnecessary expenses and finding ways to increase income.
- Seeking help from the church, family, friends, and financial advisors. Such help might include funds, or good counsel and advice. At the very least, trusted friends can pray with and for you so that you do not feel so alone.

4. Pay Off Debt Strategically

Debt can feel like a heavy burden, but with discipline and persistence, it can be managed and eliminated. **Proverbs 22:7** reminds us, *"The rich rule over the poor, and the borrower is slave to the lender."* Debt can create bondage but paying it off brings freedom.

Use strategies like the "Debt Snowball" (paying off the smallest debts first) or "Debt Avalanche" (focusing on the highest-interest debts). Communicate with creditors to negotiate payment plans or reduce interest rates. Avoid accumulating new debt during this process.

5. Seek Wise Counsel

The Bible highlights the value of seeking advice from others, especially in difficult situations. **Proverbs 15:22** says, *"Plans fail for lack of counsel, but with many advisers they succeed."* Godly counsel can provide perspective, expertise, and encouragement.

When people ask me for advice, I often warn them, "This is free advice, and worth every penny you paid for it." I'm serious when I say that, explaining that Proverbs 15:22 says, "but with MANY advisors they succeed."

Reach out to trusted mentors, church leaders, or financial counselors for advice. Consider working with a Christian financial advisor who can guide you with biblical principles. Consider their words, but also seek reach out to the MANY advisors mentioned in Proverbs 15:22.

6. Practice Contentment

Financial trouble often arises from living beyond one's means or pursuing material wealth. The Bible calls believers to be content with what they have.

I love what Paul said in **Philippians 4:12-13**: *"I know what it is to be in need, and I know what it is to have plenty. I have learned the secret of being content in any and every situation... I can do all this through him who gives me strength."* Contentment helps you focus on what truly matters and reduces financial stress.

In the Great Depression, my grandfather lost his job and became an alcoholic. There are not many family stories about him. On the other hand, there are lots of stories about my grandmother, who is said to have always been content and joyful. In the Great Depression, she made a plan, and not just one, but another and another. First, she opened her dining table to neighbors and charged them for a meal. Her neighborhood diner soon opened for breakfast, lunch, and supper. Then she started making bag lunches that the children could take to the main gate of the local textile mill and sell to workers. Next came her potato chip business. On Saturdays, the four children, including my father, helped peel, slice, and fry the potato chips. Then the kids would go from door to door selling a bag of homemade potato chips. Finally, Grandmother moved the children into the kitchen and dining room for their sleep at night, while their four bedrooms were rented out to boarders. Even Grandfather eventually joined in the work and found sobriety.

When I asked my father how bad the Great Depression had been for him, he thought for a minute and then said, "You know, it wasn't that bad. It was one of the happiest times in my life. We were together as a family, and it was great."

Finding contentment in a crisis sounds like a flippant, "suck it up," advice. But this is biblical, and you need to find some path for joy and contentment. You might find it in relationships, faith, and God's provision rather than material possessions.

7. Be Generous, Even in Difficulty

Remember the story I told earlier about the impoverished woman in India who donated a small bag of rice each Sunday so that the poor would have something to eat? The Bible encourages giving, even during hard times. Generosity demonstrates trust in God and shifts focus from personal problems to helping others.

Luke 6:38 says, *"Give, and it will be given to you. A good measure, pressed down, shaken together, and running over, will be poured into your lap."* Continue to tithe or give, even in small amounts. Volunteer your time or talents if financial giving is not possible.

8. Trust God's Provision

Financial recovery requires faith that God will provide for your needs as you work toward stability.

Matthew 6:31-33 tells us, *"So do not worry, saying, 'What shall we eat?' or 'What shall we drink?' or 'What shall we wear?' ... But seek first his kingdom and his righteousness, and all these things will be given to you as well."*

Trusting God alleviates worry and strengthens faith in His care. Focus on God's promises rather than your fears. Remember past instances of His faithfulness as encouragement for the future.

9. Move Forward with Hope
Financial trouble is not the end of the story. God specializes in redemption and restoration, even in the most difficult circumstances.

Jeremiah 29:11 says, *"For I know the plans I have for you," declares the Lord, "plans to prosper you and not to harm you, plans to give you hope and a future."*

God's plan includes hope and provision, even in financial struggles. Celebrate small victories along the way. Share your testimony of God's faithfulness to inspire others.

Conclusion: God's Faithfulness in Financial Trials
Financial trouble can feel like a storm, but God's Word provides a solid foundation for recovery. By acknowledging the problem, seeking His guidance, creating a plan, and trusting in His provision, you can overcome the challenges you face. Remember that your worth is not determined by your bank account but by your identity as a child of God. Trust Him to lead you toward restoration and peace.

As you work out of financial distress, one of the hardest things might be to be patient.

On May 25, 1961, John F. Kennedy addressed a joint session of Congress and declared that the United

States should commit itself to landing a man on the moon and returning him safely to the earth. Many people have forgotten that on May 25, 1961, America had a grand total of 15 minutes of experience in having a person in space. Just 20 days before Kennedy's speech, Alan Shephard was launched into space. It was a suborbital flight with not a single orbit around the Earth.

Kennedy's plan was to go from a tiny flight that was barely into space to landing humans on the Moon, and he gave the nation time to do this, declaring that the goal was before the end of the decade.

The goal was achieved in 1969 with Apollo 11.

You can't build a project to send humans to the moon with a mere 15 minutes of experience. But we did accomplish this in just under a decade.

Give yourself the time you need to get back on a sound financial track.

Questions for Thought

1. Do you feel you are in a challenging situation in your finances? You might be thinking about a short-term challenge, or a long-term crisis.

2. If so, have you acknowledged this situation to God in prayer?

3. Think of very trusted people with whom you might share your situation. This will not be an easy task for most. You don't want to share your finances with a gossip, or with someone who could use this information to hurt you at work or in other relationships. You want to think of people who can help mentor you and can keep a confidence.

4. Identify your sources of income. How much do you make in a typical month?

5. Identify your monthly expenses. How are you spending money on the predictable expenses, including charitable donations, rent or mortgage, power and other utilities, childcare, education, insurance, entertainment – looking at your spending look at the total of your expenses compared to your income.

6. List the things you can do without. Steaming and other online subscriptions might be cut. Daily trips to an expensive coffee shop might be reduced. Perhaps you need to shop for a different insurance plan.

7. Make a plan for debt reduction. This will take patience. Remember that it took time to get into your current situation, it will take time to get out of

it.

8. Is it time to ask family or friends for help?

9. What is it that really gives you joy, and which of these cost little or nothing? How might you continue to find joy in your life while not being overwhelmed by your debt reduction program?

Chapter 7
To Save or Not to Save:
That is NOT the Question

As a teenager, I became fascinated by the story of Joseph for many reasons. For the purposes of this book, let's ignore the sex, family dynamics, and all of the other great themes in this story from Genesis and focus on one theme in particular – saving.

To make a long story short, Joseph gives advice to Pharoah. The bad news is that a seven-year famine is coming, but the good news is that Egypt has seven years to prepare. To read more about this, look up Genesis 41:17-31. Better yet, read all of Genesis, just to be sure you get all of the sex, family dynamics, blood and gore and everything else. Why not, right? But for now, let's focus on the single theme – saving.

The seven good years are not just good years, Genesis says they are ABUNDANT years – "Seven years of great **abundance** are coming throughout the land of Egypt, but seven years of famine will follow them."

Now apply that to us.

Many of us will have years of abundance. Then the famine will come. As a pastor, I have seen people suffer when they hit retirement. Sometimes they hit a financial famine in the middle of their lives when they struggle with a serious illness. Often a parent needs help and the 40-year-old has to take on a burden. The company shuts down the mill and everyone is laid off.

Joseph is not around these days, but you can expect some years of abundance, and a few famines along the way. That's life.

The lesson of Joseph is that during the years of abundance, save and invest. Most will spend, spend, spend, spend, but <u>this</u> is the time to prepare.

Beyond the story of Joseph, we see other places where the Bible calls us to save.

Proverbs 6:6-8 says, *"Go to the ant, you <u>sluggard</u>; consider its ways and be wise! It has no commander, no overseer or ruler, yet it stores its provisions in summer and gathers its food at harvest."*

"Sluggard!" I've been called a lot of names, but no one has ever called me a sluggard. We would probably use the word "lazy" or "idle," as that is what the Hebrew word in this Old Testament verse means. Most English translations use the word "sluggard," but I like the translation of the New Living Translation here, which says, "Take a lesson from the ants, you lazybones."

I live in hurricane-prone Florida, and every year we store up provisions, as Proverbs encourages us to do. Those who live in the states north of Florida will store up for the snowy and icy conditions of winter.

Think longer term than hurricanes and ice storms. Think about a layoff, health crisis, or retirement and store up those provisions in savings and investments.

Another helpful verse is **Proverbs 21:5**, which says, *"The plans of the diligent lead to profit as surely as haste leads to poverty."* God gave you a brain, use it to plan!

Sometimes it is not the famine you will go to, you must also plan for the famine of your family. Paul wrote in **1 Timothy 5:8**: *"Anyone who does not provide for their relatives, and especially for their own household, has denied the faith and is worse than an unbeliever."*

For me, this came when an elderly relative who lived far from the rest of our family and who had no children of her own struggled after the death of her husband. My wife and I had long discussions about how we could help her and what we could do financially for her.

What about you. Do you have children with disabilities or are your parents aging with declining health? Planning means that you can provide for your family. Living paycheck to paycheck won't cut it.

The Bible also mentions many times about parents who leave an inheritance for their children. With the uncertainty of life, I may be saving for a future that never arrives. Leaving funds that will go to my son and grandson, and to my church, and other charities will require planning. **Proverbs 13:22** says, *"A good person leaves an inheritance for their children's children, but a sinner's wealth is stored up for the righteous."*

Let's also think of the Parable of the Talents. In Matthew 25:14-20, Jesus tells a story of a master who gave some servants various amounts of money, each one receiving a different sum according to ability. Everyone invested and saw the money grow, except for one who buried. It was this servant who received the wrath of the master, who told him he could have at least put it in a bank to earn interest. Saving does not mean burying cash by taping it to the back of a painting. At the very least, put the money in the bank to earn some interest, but keep in mind that is the LEAST you can do and it will not earn substantial funds for the future. Investment also needs to be part of the savings plan. You enter a world of risk, but there are conservative investments and risky investments. Your homework is to discover good investments.

Save. Invest. Prepare. But on the other hand...

The Bible encourages saving but warns against relying ONLY on those savings. One does not want to rely solely on wealth instead of trusting God. In **Matthew 6:19-21**, Jesus says, *"Do not store up for yourselves treasures on earth, where moths and vermin destroy, and where thieves break in and steal. But store up for yourselves treasures in heaven... For where your treasure is, there your heart will be also."*

A few verses later, Jesus adds in **Matthew 6:31-33**: *"So do not worry, saying, 'What shall we eat?' or 'What shall we drink?' or 'What shall we wear?' ... But seek first his kingdom and his righteousness, and all these things will be given to you as well."*

These two verses, if taken alone, would suggest that we never plan or save. But we do not take these verses alone, but rather we must here, as always, interpret a Scripture verse in light of the whole of Scripture. During the Protestant Reformation, a popular saying was, "Scripture is the best interpreter of Scripture."

That being the case, we look at these two verses with the other passages in this chapter in which we ARE encouraged to plan and save.

What are we to believe? Do we save, or do we "not store up for ourselves treasures on earth?"

We save, but we must remember that all of our savings and investments are subject to loss. A thief may steal our coin collection, or a fire can destroy our home, or the stocks may crash."

So what to do?

Plan, save, and invest, but do not trust in anything for our salvation or safety other than God Almighty. Trust in God! Someone should put that on the money! Oh wait – in the United States it IS on the money.

"In God we trust," first appeared on American currency in 1864 on a two-cent coin, using a line from the 1814 poem, "The Defense of Fort M'Henry," in which these words were found: "And this be our motto – 'In God is our trust.'" That poem was set to music to become "The Star-Spangled Banner." Eventually, the U.S. Congress adopted "In God we trust" as the official motto in 1956, replacing the still often used "E pluribus unum" (Out of many, one).

As we plan and save like Joseph in Egypt, it is not the money we trust, it is in God we trust.

In summary, what are we to do about saving?

Biblical Wisdom in Saving and Investing #1.
Saving Is Wise and Prudent.
Proverbs 6:6-8:
"Go to the ant, you sluggard; consider its ways and be wise! It has no commander, no overseer or ruler, yet it stores its provisions in summer and gathers its food at harvest."

Biblical Wisdom in Saving and Investing #2.
Providing for Family & Future Generations
1 Timothy 5:8: *"Anyone who does not provide for their relatives, and especially for their own household, has denied the faith and is worse than an unbeliever."*

Biblical Wisdom in Saving and Investing #3.
Trust God While Saving
Matthew 6:19-21: *"Do not store up for yourselves treasures on earth, where moths and vermin destroy, and where thieves break in and steal. But store up for yourselves treasures in heaven... For where your treasure is, there your heart will be also."*

Questions for Thought

1. Not all of us have the clear understanding of the future that Joseph had when he announced 7 abundant years followed by 7 lean years of famine.

However, knowing what you know, what do you need to plan for? Is it education for your children, retirement, a vacation, and the purchase of a home? Make a list of these events in your life.
2. Do you have savings and investments to cover these events?
3. How much will you need for your retirement? Decide now on a savings and investment plan. Keep in mind that many things you face can be on a "pay as you go" plan and you can take a loan on a house purchase (so you would only need to save for your down payment). You cannot use loans to fund your retirement.
4. How much do you have for your emergency fund to cover a new roof, appliance replacement, or other emergencies?
5. About that emergency fund – take your monthly income and multiply it by 6 to 10. A six to ten month emergency fund is what you need. Are you on target, or do you need more? How will you get there?

Chapter 8
Money and Marriage

Many of the couples in my church seemed to have perfect marriages. They seemed to have it all together.

As the pastor, I would eventually get a deeper glimpse into these perfect marriages. One or both of the partners would come to me as their pastor and share the stress and pain in which they were struggling. The main points of stress seemed to involve one or more of the following:

- Financial problems
- Sex
- Family issues
- Different expectations of what marriage should be
- Child-related issues
- Employment pressures

And did I mention finances?

Money is one of the most significant and sensitive aspects of any marriage. It has the power to unite or divide, strengthen or weaken. The Bible provides profound wisdom for couples to handle money in a way that fosters unity, trust, and godliness. Since this book focuses on biblical money management, we will ignore the other stress points in marriage and focus only on money. This is not to suggest that the others are not worthy of one's time and consideration, but rather in this book, our focus is money.

What can the Bible teach the married couple about money management?

1. Marriage as a Partnership
In thinking about money within a marriage, understand that marriage is designed to be a union where two become one (Genesis 2:24). This applies not only to the emotional and spiritual aspects of the relationship but also to practical matters like finances. The Bible encourages couples to work together, supporting one another and sharing burdens.

There is a wonderful passage in **Ecclesiastes 4:9-12:** *"Two are better than one, because they have a good return for their labor: If either of them falls down, one can help the other up. But pity anyone who falls and has no one to help them up. Also, if two lie down together, they will keep warm. But how can one keep warm alone? Though one may be overpowered, two can defend themselves."*

In marriage, two people enter a covenant in which they will be there for each other. They support each other. The "have each other's back." They stand up for each other.

In preparing to conduct a wedding for a couple, I usually know one, but not the other. I always start our first meeting in wedding counseling with my asking, "Tell me how you two met." I do this because one, or both, are nervous when they come into the pastor's office. When I ask this question, I'm asking the couple to tell me a story that they know well, and have often told, so they relax and tell wonderful stories.

In one case, I had known the groom since he was a young child, but I had never met the bride.

Together they told this great tale. It seems that Mike had a back spasm. To solve it, he thought it would be a good idea to use a new back massage chair to work out the kinks. Well, like many men, Mike ignored the warning label that told him not to use it for more than 15 minutes. After an hour of relaxation, his back completely seized up. Mike described it as feeling like being stabbed with a long sword. I'm not sure how Mike came to be familiar with what it is like to be stabbed with a sword, but I took him at his word.

Mike was able to make it to the bed – but not actually onto the bed, but with his head on the bed and his legs hanging off the bed he stayed in a horrible position for three hours. He was able to reach his phone in his pocket and get a message to Ali, whom he barely knew and with whom he had gone on a first date very recently.

This was the only contact he had on his brand new phone. For reasons Mike did not understand, his new phone had trouble syncing with the old phone, and he was still trying to get his old contacts onto the new phone.

Poor Mike. He was alone, in distress, and had only one contact on his phone. He was in pain, and unable to get up. Mike was desperate for relief – and not just relief from pain. The poor guy was half-way in bed for three hours, and before that in a massage chair for an hour.

His bladder was pretty full.

He had no one else to whom he could go for help, so he called Ali, who came to his rescue. While Ali is holding a plastic bucket so Mike could urinate, he has an epiphany– "this is the woman for me!"

When I have asked couples when they knew they were meant for each other, their story was the <u>least</u> romantic answer I had ever heard! But --- it remains the <u>best</u> answer I have ever heard.

Wrapped up in that story is the essence of what real marriage is about. Yes, marriage is about sex and romance and joy and love, love, lots of love. It is sometimes about children and success and great moments. And it is about pain, humiliating experiences, and agony. And being there in the best of life, and in the worst of life. And it is in the worst moments when the true essence of marriage is discovered. Marriage exists so that two people enter a lasting covenant so they will be there for each other.

This brings us to **Marriage and Money Principle #1: Money management in marriage is stronger when both partners work together.**
Shared goals, open communication, and mutual support create a foundation that withstands financial challenges.

Couples should regularly discuss financial goals, budgets, and decisions, recognizing that their combined efforts yield better results than working independently.

<u>Marriage and Money Principle #2.</u> Communicate Openly About Finances
Money is often a source of conflict in marriage, but many issues arise from poor communication. The Bible emphasizes honesty and transparency in relationships.

Proverbs 27:23 says: *"Be sure you know the condition of your flocks, give careful attention to your herds."*

Apply that verse to your finances. Brenda came to me one day and was very angry. She was approaching retirement. Her husband had died a few months earlier. They had never discussed finances. She knew that she was the beneficiary of his retirement funds. Together they had joint ownership of some mutual funds. But she had never had any interest in these matters and left all decisions to her husband. She was shocked to learn that her financial resources had been diminished.

Proverbs 27:23 would have informed them that both the husband and the wife should have known the condition of their flocks. They didn't have sheep, but they did have investments, and the wisdom and principle of Proverbs still applied to the 21st Century.

Even if one spouse is more skillful than the other in making decisions, both should be well informed and have a say at what happens to their "flock" of funds. Set aside time for honest conversations about income, expenses, debts, and savings. Avoid secrecy or unilateral decisions that could lead to mistrust.

Marriage and Money Principle #3: Create a Shared Budget and Financial Goals

A budget is a practical tool for stewardship and a way to ensure that financial priorities align with God's will. There is a great line in **Luke 14:28-30**: *"Suppose one of you wants to build a tower. Won't you first sit down and estimate the cost to see if you have enough money to complete it?"* Wise financial planning is essential for achieving goals. Work together to create a budget that reflects your values and goals. Include tithing, saving, and giving as part of your plan.

Marriage and Money Principle #4: Practice Generosity Together

Generosity is a hallmark of Christian stewardship. When couples give together, they grow closer and demonstrate trust in God. Paul says in **2 Corinthians 9:7**: *"Each of you should give what you have decided in your heart to give, not reluctantly or under compulsion, for God loves a cheerful giver."* Notice that Paul is advising that we give what we "have decided," which implies discussion, thought, research, and planning. In a marriage, giving reflects a shared commitment to God's kingdom and the needs of others. Couples need to agree on how much and where to give. Whether it's supporting your church, missions, or helping the needy, generosity strengthens your bond as a couple.

Marriage and Money Principle #5: Trust God in Financial Challenges

Financial difficulties are inevitable, but they are also opportunities for growth in faith and unity. Howard Clinebell was one of my teachers in pastoral counseling, and I have always remembered one of his comments: "Life crises, both accidental and developmental, can be used as opportunities for growth if persons encounter them in a context of meaning and within the loving support of a network of caring."

In other words, a crisis is an opportunity for growth. A financial crisis in marriage is an opportunity to grow in a couple's ability to trust in God.

Paul wrote in **Philippians 4:19**: *"My God will meet all your needs according to the riches of his glory in Christ Jesus."* Trusting God provides peace and strength during financial trials. Couples need to pray together about financial challenges, seek wisdom from Scripture, and rely on God's provision rather than worrying or blaming each other.

Marriage and Money Principle #6: Avoid Debt and Financial Strain

One of the major sources of financial stress in a marriage comes from debt. This is especially dangerous to a marriage when one partner is the source of all or most of the debt. This is also a reason why couples need to share all financial information with each other.

We have already devoted a chapter on this principle regarding debt. I won't repeat the whole of that chapter, but I do find it worth repeating this one particular verse as a reminder. **Proverbs 22:7**: *"The rich rule over the poor, and the borrower is slave to the lender."*

Debt can create unnecessary burdens and strain on a marriage. Agree to live within your means, or as my wife and I like to say to other couples, "live BENEATH your means. Avoid unnecessary debt and work together to pay off existing debts.

Marriage and Money Principle #7: Prepare to Die!

I could probably say this more pleasantly, but I want to be clear. A successful marriage ends in death. Remember the words of your wedding? There was probably a line that read, "Until death do you part."

I had a couple in my church and when the husband died, the wife had no idea where the life insurance policies were, or even if they had insurance. She did not know how to contact the husband's pension, or if those payments would continue to be available to her as a surviving spouse. She had no idea how much her Social Security was, or her husband's.

My wife and I know exactly where our "end of life" documents are located. My son also knows, and I think I have probably taken one too many opportunities to let him know, because the last time I told him he interrupted me, saying, "Yes, yes, I know. The dead daddy stuff is in the cabinet where the useless China dishes are kept, wrapped up in the Zip Lock bag that you bought right after plastic was invented during the American Civil War."

There is nothing wrong with letting the folks who will need to know where these things are and letting them know so many times they get tired of it. Besides, after his last comment about the dead daddy stuff makes me look forward with what he will come up with next!

So, what should be in the end of life documents?

Your will. When I am asked to conduct a baptism for a child, I ask the parents, "do you have a will." Almost always the answer is "no," to which I always respond, "Actually, you do have a will. The State of Florida will be happy to decide who raises your child in the event of your death, and we know that we can always trust the government to do what is best for us." Get a will, and also consider a trust. This is where I remind you that I am a biblical scholar, not a financial expert. Go somewhere else besides this book for this legal advice. Find a lawyer who can help you with estate planning.

A durable power of attorney for finances names someone who will make financial decisions for you when you are unable to. Again, a lawyer can help you with this.

A living trust names and instructs a person, called the trustee, to hold and distribute property and funds on your behalf when you are no longer able to manage your affairs.

A living will tells doctors how you want to be treated if you cannot make your own decisions about emergency treatment. You can say which common medical treatments or care you would want, which ones you would want to avoid, and under which conditions each of your choices applies.

Advance Care Documents, such as a durable power of attorney for health. This document names your health care proxy, a person who can make health care decisions for you if you are unable to communicate these yourself. Your proxy — also known as a representative, surrogate, or agent — should be familiar with your values and wishes. A proxy can be chosen in addition to or instead of a living will. Having a healthcare proxy helps you plan for situations that cannot be foreseen, such as a serious auto accident or stroke.

Put your important papers and copies of legal documents in one place. You can set up a file, put everything in a desk or a dresser drawer, or list the information and location of papers in a notebook.

General information should be in this accessible place with the other documents. These include:
Personal information
- Full legal name
- Social Security number
- Legal residence
- Date and place of birth
- Names and addresses of spouse and children
- Location of birth and death certificates and certificates of marriage, divorce, citizenship, and adoption
- Employers and dates of employment
- Education and military records
- Names and phone numbers of religious contacts
- Memberships in groups and awards received

- Names and phone numbers of close friends, relatives, doctors, lawyers, and financial advisors

Financial information
- Sources of income and assets (pension from your employer, IRAs, 401(k)s, interest, etc.)
- Social Security information
- Insurance information (life, long-term care, home, car) with policy numbers and agents' names and phone numbers
- Names of your banks and account numbers (checking, savings, credit union)
- Investment income (stocks, bonds, property) and stockbrokers' names and phone numbers
- Copy of the most recent income tax return
- Location of most up-to-date will with an original signature
- Liabilities, including property tax, mortgages and other debts
- Location of original deed of trust for home
- Car title and registration
- Credit and debit card names and numbers
- Location of safe deposit box and key

Health information
- Current prescriptions (be sure to update this regularly)
- Living will
- Durable power of attorney for health care
- Copies of any medical orders or forms you have (for example, a do-not-resuscitate order)
- Health insurance information with policy and phone numbers

Review your plans regularly. It's important to review your plans at least once each year and when any major life event occurs, like a divorce, move, or major change in your health. I generally review annually what my son calls the "dead daddy stuff" that I keep in the world's oldest Zip Lock bag. For me, that is done after I finish my tax returns. I choose that time because in my "dead daddy" stuff is a printout of the most recent tax files, so it is a good time to go through everything.

Conclusion: United in Finances and Faith

Money management in marriage is not just about numbers—it's about partnership, trust, and honoring God. By following biblical principles, couples can strengthen their relationship and reflect God's design for unity. Remember Ecclesiastes 4:12: *"A cord of three strands is not quickly broken."* When Christ is the center of your marriage, even financial challenges become opportunities to grow closer to each other and to God.

Questions for Thought

1. How well do you and your spouse work in harmony with family money management?

2. How much do each of you communicate about finances?

3. Does each spouse know where accounts are and how to access them?

4. With your spouse, talk about your income and expenses, and work out a budget both can agree on.

5. Spend some time talking about the debts you have jointly and individually.

6. In the event death, does the surviving spouse know all that he or she needs to know about handling finances alone? Are the financial papers, deeds, wills, accounts, insurance policies and all of the other important documents in places of easy access to the survivor?

Chapter 9
The Gift and Nature of Work

As a pastor, I have noticed how people respond differently to work. Some love it, some hate it. Some do it well, and others do it poorly.

I loved most of the jobs I've had. My first job was to work as a child model for J. C. Penney's. I was in the 2nd Grade and found it humiliating to walk onto a stage while some grown up described my dorky hat and suit as "delightful" and lied about how I'd be the envy of all my classmates, knowing full well I'd be bullied on the playground. I also found it confusing that I was sitting on Santa's lap for photos in the middle of April while a photographer took pictures for the Christmas catalog.

My work as a pastor involved long hours and was often difficult, but it was so rewarding. I certainly did not enjoy conducting funerals after a tragic death, but I felt it was worthwhile to the family. I was working for one of the greatest organizations on the planet – the church. As Pastor J. John puts it, this is a global enterprise with outlets in nearly every country in the world. We have hospitals, and hospices, and homeless shelters. We do marriage counseling, career counseling, and we are involved in justice reconciliation. We work with people from birth to death and we deal in the area of behavior modification.

Working as a "lint head" in a textile mill was always agonizing. The clock moved too slowly. It was monotonous. I gave up trying to get the cotton lint out of my hair and I worried about what that would do to my lungs. The only good thing that I can say is that the paycheck was regular and helped me get through my last semester in college.

But I did like the money!

This is not to say that the only job I had that I loved was ministry. I loved being a sports photographer for a newspaper. Working in a state prison was never dull. When I worked in kitchens, I had no idea I was preparing for a life-long love for cooking for my family and friends. After I retired from ministry, I worked as an astronomer which was a pure delight.

How have you felt about your jobs? More importantly, how do you feel about your present job?

The book of **Ecclesiastes** in the Bible reflects on the value of work from a philosophical and spiritual perspective, often grappling with its meaning in the grand scheme of life. Two passages from Ecclesiastes addresses how work can feel oppressive and futile without a larger purpose. In **Ecclesiastes 1:3** we read, *"What do people gain from all their labors at which they toil under the sun?"* Keep in mind that the author of Ecclesiastes is an old man who has the benefit of being able to look back on his life.

That is an excellent question, and the writer of this book repeats it, this time with an answer. In **Ecclesiastes**

2:22-35 we read this: *"What do people get for all the toil and anxious striving with which they labor under the sun? All their days their work is grief and pain; even at night their minds do not rest. This too is meaningless. A person can do nothing better than to eat and drink and find satisfaction in their own work. This too, I see, is from the hand of God, for without him, who can eat or find enjoyment?"* While work can seem meaningless in isolation, the writer acknowledges that finding joy in work is a blessing from God.

This is such an excellent idea, that the writer repeats it in **Ecclesiastes 3:13**: *"That each of them may eat and drink and find satisfaction in all their work—this is the gift of God."* What a blessing to find joy and satisfaction in one's work.

I once had a conversation with a young man in my church. He was about to start college, and I asked about his long-term goals.

"I don't care what I do for work, as long as I make a lot of money and have the weekend off."

I suggested that from Monday through Friday, most of his day would be spent working, so wouldn't it be nice to have a job he enjoyed? He disagreed. The goal of work is to make money.

True, that is part of the goal, but what's better is to have a job that fills you with satisfaction and joy. Good advice to that young man, and to all those looking for a first job or a change in work comes again from **Ecclesiastes 9:10**, *"Whatever your hand finds to do, do it with all your* *might."*

The Bible encourages wholehearted engagement in work. I have my great grandfather's diary. He came to this country in 1877 and worked for the rest of his life as a gardener. His diary is full of meteorological observations and schedule of planting. He wrote with joy about watching the tulips begin to grow and bloom. He took enormous satisfaction in his hard work.

Work is a gift from God, designed to provide for our needs, shape our character, and contribute to His purposes. In the Bible, work and wealth are interconnected, not as ends in themselves, but as tools for stewardship and service.

Even when I was working as a "lint head" in a textile mill, glancing often at the clock as if that would make time move more quickly, I earnestly tried to take some satisfaction from a joyless job, and to do it to God's glory. I had been moved by St. Paul's words in **Colossians 3:23-24**: *"Whatever you do, work at it with all your heart, as working for the Lord, not for human masters, since you know that you will receive an inheritance from the Lord as a reward. It is the Lord Christ you are serving."*

Work is not just about earning money; it is an act of worship and service to God. Every task, no matter how mundane, can be done for His glory. Knowing that can bring glimpses of joy even to a lint head.

While the Bible affirms the value of hard work, it also warns against overwork and neglecting rest. God designed a rhythm of work and rest, demonstrating this in the Ten Commandments. **Exodus 20:9-10** says that we are to work six days and do all our work, "B*ut the seventh day is a sabbath to the Lord your God. On it you shall not do any work."* God himself presented this in the first creation account of Genesis, which ends with Genesis 2:2-3: *"On the seventh day God ended His work which He had done, and He rested on the seventh day from all His work which He had done. Then God blessed the seventh day and sanctified it, because in it He rested from all His work which God had created and made."*

God's command to rest reminds us that we are not defined by our productivity and that ultimate provision comes from Him. You must schedule regular times of rest to recharge physically, emotionally, and spiritually. Be intentional about planning a day of rest by honoring the Sabbath.

As a pastor, I watched many people working at the church who were volunteers, giving up their time off, or even their day off to work with me. If they wanted to meet with me on a Friday or Saturday, they would not respond well if I suggested another day, as Friday and Saturdays were my usual days off. Some were indignant, saying, "But I'm willing to give up my day off." I learned early to simply say, "I'm booked that day," and leave it at that. I had to schedule my days off and be intentional about it. Only a wedding or funeral would lead me to reschedule. As a pastor, I knew that I could not do my best if I allowed myself to become overworked and fatigued.

We must all be intentional and guard your time of rest. Protect your time off and find ways to relax and renew yourself.

Work and rest are gifts from God, meant to be approached with diligence, balance, and a heart of service. By working hard, resting wisely, and trusting in God's provision, we honor Him in our labor and reflect His glory in the world. Let us embrace every task as an act of worship, remembering the words of **Colossians 3:23**: *"Whatever you do, work at it with all your heart, as working for the Lord, not for human masters."*

Questions for Thought

1. What was your favorite job, and what made it a good experience?

2. What was your least favorite job, and what made it an unpleasant job?

3. How would you evaluate your current job? Are you getting out of it, and putting into it, what you desire?

4. Are their changes you need to make to make your current job a better place for you?

5. If you would could envision the ideal job for you, what would it be?

Chapter 10
A Hard Financial Skill to Learn: Patience

An elder came into my office one day, very excited about a new book he had read – WEALTH WITHOUT RISK by Charles J. Givens. When I say "elder" I am referring to an ordained position in the church, not an age. He and I were both in our 30s.

"This book is going to change our lives," he told me, and it did. It is now out of print, and I suspect a lot of the information is out of date. But at the time, this book guided me in the purchase of my first home, helped me save on my car insurance, and taught me how to invest money.

I invested $500 right away and started automatically sending $25 each month to an index stock fund. Whenever I got a raise, that $25 increased. At the end of the first year, I had less than $1,000. A few years later, I had $30,000. I remember how excited I was when I passed the $100,000 mark. I eventually invested much more than $25 per month. By the time my grandson was born, I had quite a nice nest egg saved up and I still had time before retirement.

Financial advisors would see that I was taking advantage of "dollar cost averaging" and "compound interest."

Theologically, I was demonstrating the biblical call to have a plan, and to have patience.

Patience is not merely a virtue but a necessity in both spiritual and financial matters. The Bible teaches the value of waiting on God's timing and exercising restraint, two qualities essential to successful money management. **Proverbs 21:5** tells us, *"The plans of the diligent lead surely to abundance, but everyone who is hasty comes only to poverty."* This verse underscores the profound importance of patience in making sound financial decisions and realizing long-term goals. In this chapter, we will explore how patience, as a biblical principle, can guide wise money management and amplify the benefits of a compound interest strategy.

Another great passage to consider is **James 5:7-8** - *"Be patient, therefore, brothers, until the coming of the Lord. See how the farmer waits for the precious fruit of the earth, being patient about it, until it receives the early and the late rains."* Like the farmer, investors and savers must exercise patience to reap financial rewards.

The Old Testament verse that presents better than most how important patience is in financial management is **Proverbs 13:11** - *"Wealth gained hastily will dwindle, but whoever gathers little by little will increase it."*

Let's pause and define two terms you've read in this chapter. You may or may not be familiar with these terms: "dollar cost averaging," and "compound interest."

Let's say you open a stock fund account and invest $100 into that fund every month. If the market goes up, you are buying less shares, but when the market goes down, you buy more shares. That is dollar cost averaging. Over time, this strategy could lower your average cost per share compared to what you would have paid if you'd bought all your shares at once when they were more expensive than the average.

When I was in high school, we were taught one of the secrets of investing in the stock market was "buy low, sell high." That makes sense, but if you are investing on a regular basis, it is stressful. Do you invest when the price is high, or wait until it comes down again? If you set up your accounts so that the bank automatically sends that $100 to your stock fund every month, then you should come out a winner over time, thanks to "dollar cost averaging."

Now let's look at the second term, "compound interest." When you save or invest, your money earns interest, dividends, or appreciates. The next year, you earn interest on your original money *and* the interest from the first year. In the third year, you earn interest on your original money and the interest on the income from those first *two* years. This goes on and on so that your money is growing like a snowball, getting larger and larger.

Take a look at John, who is a 22-year-old college graduate. He puts $300 per month into a stock fund account earning 10% per year for six years. That's the average annual return of the stock market over time. Six years later, John is 28 years old and is married, has kids, and a mortgage, and can no longer invest $300 every month. By that time, John has invested $21,600 of his own money. If he never contributes another cent, his money would grow into a million dollars by the time he turned 65. That is the secret of compound interest AND the biblical practice of patience.

Now look at Jane. She put off saving until she was 31. She can still become a millionaire, but it will be more difficult. She would have to contribute the same $300 every month but instead of 6 years, it would be for the next 34 years to earn $1 million by age 65.

John invested less money out-of-pocket -- $21,600 over six years. Jane invested $126,000 over 34 years. John's money had more time to grow or compound. Patience!

For both John and Jane, the money is invested at a regular disciplined rate, but when each stops investing they are patient and kept their hands off their money. In that way it continued to grow and grow.

Even a little goes a long way. Take Amy who opened a stock fund account at the age of 20. She put in $50 every month, which is more affordable than the $300 Jane and John invested. Let's say she still earns 10% annually, as that is the average the stock market has grown over time. At the age of 65 she has $528,000.

Amy retires at the age of 65 and she takes out only the income from the fund, leaving the principle alone. If the income stays at 10% per year, what is that income?

528,000 × 0.10 =52,800

Take that $52,800 and divide into 12 monthly payments, and Amy will have $4,400 per month in income. But wait, there's more! She will also have Social Security payments and perhaps pension as well.

She is being blessed with what the world calls dollar cost averaging, and compound interest – or what the Bible calls a plan and patience.

Let me stop here and admit that this sounds like a chapter from a lot of books written by financial gurus. That's true, but the values of dollar cost averaging and compound interest are universally acknowledged. They also go hand in hand with my area of expertise, which is not financial management, but biblical studies – discipline and patience.

There are many other things to consider. Where will you put your money? A bank account will pay far less than 10%. Stocks can be purchased individually, or in mutual funds. Mutual funds come in all sorts of varieties focusing on different issues. The best bet for many is to look at a Roth IRA (Individual Retirement Account), which is an index fund, which reflects the rise and fall of the Dow Stock Index or other indices. A financial advisor may be your best source of information.

Remember **Proverbs 11:14**, which says, "For lack of guidance a nation falls, but victory is won through many advisers." An almost identical verse makes this more personal: **Proverbs 15:22** says "Plans fail for lack of counsel, but with many advisers they succeed." Consider me your advisor on biblical studies – now go out and find a financial advisor.

It would be best to go to a financial advisor who is a "fiduciary." The main difference between a financial advisor and a fiduciary financial advisor lies in the legal and ethical obligation they have toward their clients. A financial advisor may do a fine job, but one who is a certified fiduciary will have your best interest at heart.

Conclusion
Patience, as modeled in Scripture, is a vital skill for managing money wisely. It helps us resist the allure of instant gratification, navigate challenges with resilience, and experience the full rewards of our efforts over time. When paired with the principle of compound interest, patience becomes a powerful tool for building wealth in a way that honors God.

In the end, biblical money management is not just about accumulating wealth but stewarding it faithfully for God's glory. By cultivating patience, we not only achieve financial success but also grow in character, faith, and trust in the Lord's perfect timing.

Questions for Thought

1. Think of a time when you had to be patient for a desired outcome. How did you find the patience to see you through?

2. As you think about meeting your financial goals, what are the things that you need to be patient about? How can you create and nurture the patience you need?

Chapter 11
Good at Any Age – Thrifty Living

I'm not sure what brought it up, but one day I was visiting my Dad and I mentioned how some passages of the Bible did not make any sense, and I gave him what I thought was the perfect example. **Leviticus 19:19** prohibits mixing different fibers. I love 100% cotton, but I have a lot of clothing that is 50% this and another 50% of that. What's the problem?

My Dad was a textile executive who had never heard of this passage, but he understood it immediately. Different fibers shrink at different rates. Today we preshrink fibers, so it is not a major issue, but in ancient times if you wove two different fibers they would rip apart. It was a waste of resources. No thrifty person would weave together different materials for a garment you could only wash once.

And there it was – thrift! It was the answer to Leviticus 19:19 and the answer to a lot of financial woe. Money, like any resource, is a gift from God. As stewards of God's blessings, we are called to manage our finances with care, wisdom, and responsibility. One of the most practical ways to honor God with our finances is by embracing

thriftiness—the discipline of living within our means, avoiding waste, and maximizing the value of what we have.

Thriftiness is not about being miserly or stingy; instead, it reflects a heart that recognizes the value of resources and seeks to use them for God's glory and the good of others. Scripture offers profound wisdom on this subject, guiding us to live lives of financial prudence and intentionality.

Let's consider several passages in which the Bible speaks of thriftiness. What can we learn from them?

Thrifty people tend to plan and consider costs, while others spend recklessly. In **Luke 14:28-30** we read, *"Suppose one of you wants to build a tower. Won't you first sit down and estimate the cost to see if you have enough money to complete it? For if you lay the foundation and are not able to finish it, everyone who sees it will ridicule you."* We have mentioned this passage before and considered its application to plan ahead. The verse is also about considering the cost and whether you have enough to complete a project. This reflects the biblical value on the importance of planning and budgeting before undertaking projects.

Where are you in this? Forget the tower, which most of you will not plan on building. Think of the meals you will serve in your home. "Won't you first sit down and estimate the cost," as Jesus suggests in Luke? Estimating the cost will look at sales and thrift. Planning for college, buying a house, and buying a car are all projects like planning to build a tower in Luke.

I've bought and sold several cars in my lifetime. I have noticed that car dealers often steer me to these wonderful vehicles that have all the great technology, bells and whistles. But if I bought them, I'd have to struggle to afford the gas to put into the car so I could go places. A less expensive car would fit in with the balance of my life.

Jesus practiced thrift, and we can see this in **John 6:12** - *"When they had all had enough to eat, he said to his disciples, 'Gather the pieces that are left over. Let nothing be wasted.'"*

We practice this in my family when we gather at my home for a meal. After the meal, we gather food that is left so that it will go home with different folks and be enjoyed the next day. Nothing should go to waste in a thrifty home.

Perhaps the best lesson in being thrifty is the Parable of the Prodigal Son. First, many people misunderstand the term "prodigal," thinking it refers to someone who comes to their senses and returns home and to family. Or they associate the word "prodigal" with "repentant."

No. The word "prodigal" means wasteful.

Its origins come from the 1500s and probably comes from the French word "prodigal," meaning extravagant, or from the Latin "prodigus," meaning wasteful.

We have looked at that parable in a previous chapter as we considered how to deal with being in financial troubles. Let's look at it again with the thought of being thrifty rather than wasteful. The Parable of the Prodigal Son is told in **Luke 15:11-31.**

Jesus continued: "There was a man who had two sons. [12] The younger one said to his father, 'Father, give me my share of the estate.' So, he divided his property between them.

[13] *"Not long after that, the younger son got together all he had, set off for a distant country and there squandered his wealth in wild living. [14] After he had spent everything, there was a severe famine in that whole country, and he began to be in need. [15] So he went and hired himself out to a citizen of that country, who sent him to his fields to feed pigs. [16] He longed to fill his stomach with the pods that the pigs were eating, but no one gave him anything.*

This illustrates the danger of prodigal, or wasteful, choices. It is contrary to being thrifty. Not only does he waste his fortune, this son also wastes his relationship with his family. Fortunately, when the son decides to go back to his father to offer himself up as a hired hand, the father welcomes him with loving and open arms. But not every story of a prodigal person ends up so well.

A good example of a bad ending to a life lacking thrift comes from the F. Scott Fitzgerald novel, "The Great Gatsby." Taking place in the 1920s, the fictional Jay Gatsby and others in the novel, squandered their wealth. But a similar story of waste can be seen in the writer himself. Fitzgerald enjoyed early success as a writer and earned significant income through his novels and short stories. At his peak, he was a celebrated literary figure and part of the Jazz Age elite. However, he and his wife Zelda led an extravagant lifestyle. They lived far beyond their means, borrowed money, saved little, and fell deeply into debt. At the young age of 44, Fitzgerald died of coronary disease, probably due to the stress of his financial situation and his alcoholism.

Conclusion: Thriftiness as a Spiritual Discipline

Thriftiness is more than a financial practice—it is a spiritual discipline that reflects our trust in God, gratitude for His provision, and commitment to stewarding His resources wisely. By embracing thriftiness, we free ourselves from the pressures of materialism, build financial stability, and create opportunities for generosity.

As you consider your financial habits, ask yourself:
- Am I honoring God with how I use my resources?
- How can I live more simply and save more effectively?
- What steps can I take today to embrace thriftiness and glorify God with my finances?

Through thriftiness, we not only strengthen our financial health but also deepen our faith, learning to rely on God as our ultimate Provider and source of true wealth.

Questions for Thought

1. Everyone has a personal culture or psychology of money. Some will spend money as it comes in, others are avid savers. Some spend more than they

bring in, others are hoarders. How would you describe your approach to money as it is right now?

2. Is this the approach you want to have, or would you want to have a different approach to money?

3. Think about your childhood and youth. How did your experiences growing up influence your approach to money? Did it make you careful or careless, a saver or a spender? Do you want to embrace, or move beyond how your growing up shaped your approach to money?

Chapter 12
Finding Contentment and Peace With What You Have

"Tin Can" was a homeless man whom I met when I was the pastor of the Chapel by the Sea on Fort Myers Beach, Florida. As the pastor, I was also responsible for a program we called "God's Table," which fed and assisted those in need on our island. Like most homeless people on the beach, he had a nickname. He'd earned his by collecting soda cans, which he was able to recycle for a small price.

He had very little, but he was among the most contented people I have ever met. He would come to Chapel by the Sea for the breakfast served by God's Table. He would arrive early to help set up, and then he would stay late to clean up. He was never in a hurry. He would borrow one of the church's fishing poles we kept for the homeless and catch fresh fish for lunch. When we added a few cast nets to be available to borrow, he was able to enjoy shrimp for dinner. What a great life - living on an island in the Gulf of Mexico and dining on the best and freshest seafood. Thanks to Tin Can, God's Table was often serving shrimp cocktails for breakfast.

Tourists paid top dollar for a few days of such a life and Tin Can enjoyed it year-round.

Douglas, on the other hand, had everything. Like many of the parishioners at Chapel by the Sea, he was a retired businessman. Chapel was full of former CEO's, CFO's, and other business leaders. Douglas had a home on our beach for the winters, but another in Canada for the summers, and wonderful sailboat. But he was miserable and tense. He once admitted to me that he was jealous of what Tin Can had.

One does not find contentment in money, nor does one find it in poverty. It is found in knowing what your true treasures are.

Contentment is a cornerstone of biblical financial management. In a world that constantly urges us to acquire more, the Bible calls us to find peace in God's provision. Contentment is not about complacency but about aligning our desires with God's will and trusting Him for our needs.

Beware of the Dangers of Greed

We have already devoted an entire chapter on the dangers of Greed. The Bible repeatedly warns against the love of money and the endless pursuit of material possessions. Greed can lead to spiritual destruction, strained relationships, and misplaced priorities.

Once again, I will repeat a verse we've shared earlier. It is a warning from **Ecclesiastes 5:10**, "*Whoever* *loves money never has enough; whoever loves wealth is never satisfied with their income."*

Greed, if we allow it into our hearts, will prevent us from experiencing the contentment of having enough.

Cultivating Contentment in a Consumer-Driven World

Contentment is not a natural state—it is a discipline and a fruit of trusting God. The apostle Paul provides a powerful example of contentment in all circumstances. In **Philippians 4:11-13** he writes, *"I am not saying this because I am in need, for I have learned to be content whatever the circumstances. I know what it is to be in need, and I know what it is to have plenty. I have learned the secret of being content in any and every situation, whether well fed or hungry, whether living in plenty or in want. I can do all this through him who gives me strength."*

Notice that Paul did not say he was given the **gift** of contentment, but rather this is something he learned. When I was in the third grade, my teacher said with great aggravation, "Oh if I could just open your heads and pour in the knowledge, I would. But I can't. You have to study, work, and practice in order to learn." If you thought learning algebra or history were tough, why would you think learning contentment would be easy? It's hard work and takes time.

Contentment is learned through reliance on Christ, not through material abundance. Here are a few practical steps to learning to be content in all situations.

1. **Shift Your Focus to Eternal Values:**
    - Reflect on Matthew 6:19-21. In this passage, Jesus says *"Do not store up for yourselves treasures on earth, where moths and pests destroy, and where thieves break in and steal. But store up for yourselves treasures in heaven, where moths and pests do not destroy, and where thieves do not break in and steal."* In the very next verse, there is this great line: *"For where your treasure is, there your heart will be also."* If you are trying to learn contentment, you need to ask, "What is my treasure?" Is it my car? Is it my jewelry? Is it my net worth? Is it my spouse, kids, and friendship?

    - Regularly evaluate how your financial decisions align with God's purposes. Are you taking care of people around you who are in need? Are you caring for your family?

2. **Practice Gratitude:**

    - Make a habit of thanking God daily for His provision, both big and small.

    - Focus on what you have rather than what you lack.

3. **Limit Exposure to Consumerism:**

    - I have a personal rule that prohibits buying anything I see while standing in line at the grocery store. I don't need that candy bar or magazine. Lately, I've realized that advertisements on social media are mysteriously aligned with my interests. Standing against the task master of consumerism can free us from the slavery of wanting more and more "stuff."

- Resist impulse buying by adopting a 24-hour rule before making non-essential purchases.

4. **Simplify Your Lifestyle:**

    - Declutter your home and donate items you no longer use.

    - Choose quality over quantity in your spending habits.

    - "If I haven't used it in a year, I throw it out," may work for you, but not for me. There are things I use every other year. Living in Florida means I have a generator, and other hurricane supplies I hope I use only every few years, but when I need them, I really need them! There is no "one size fits all rule," but you need to start thinking about what will work for you.

5. **Trust God's Provision:**

    - Reflect on **Matthew 6:31-33**, which says, *"So do not worry, saying, 'What shall we eat?' or 'What shall we drink?' or 'What shall we wear?' For the godless run after all* *these things, and your heavenly Father knows that you need them. But seek first his kingdom and his righteousness, and all these things will be given to you as well."* This verse encourages trust in God for daily needs. There are times when I wonder if this works for even the poor, but I always decide it works for both the poor and rich. This verse teaches all of us to trust in God, like it says on the American money, and not so much to trust in ourselves or our investments. Trust in God is the pathway toward contentment.

Conclusion: Finding Peace in Christ

Contentment is not about what you have. It is about who you trust. When we place our trust in God rather than wealth, we experience peace that surpasses understanding. Remember Paul's words in **Philippians 4:13:** *"I can do all this through him who gives me strength."*

By cultivating contentment, practicing gratitude, and managing money biblically, we can honor God with our resources and live in the freedom He desires for us.

Questions for Thought

1. Think back on a time when you experienced a time of great contentment. What was it like? Why were you so contented in that memory?

2. Remember a time when you were very discontented. What contributed to your distress? Have you found contentment again, and if so, how?

3. What about your finances robs you of contentment and joy? What can you do about those impairments?

Chapter 13
Homework!
Listening to the Secular Counsel

Psalm 15:22 says, *"Without counsel plans fail, but with many advisers they succeed."* This is not the first time you have read this verse in this book. I am one counsel among the many you should be seeking. I have been clear that I am not a financial advisor, but a biblical scholar focusing on the wisdom the Scripture offers in money management. I implore you to listen to the biblical wisdom, but I also urge you to listen to secular wisdom. This is your homework!

Throughout this book, we have explored biblical wisdom on managing money—principles rooted in discipline, stewardship, and intentionality. However, effectively managing your money in the modern world also requires practical, actionable steps based on proven strategies. By combining timeless, biblical values with modern financial tools, anyone can improve their financial present and future.

Because this book is focused on what Scripture leads us to believe and do, I will not give you extensive advice on the secular instructions. That is your homework.

These are the things you need to study on your own and continue to seek the counsel of the many.

1. The Power of Dollar-Cost Averaging

What It Is: Dollar-cost averaging (DCA) is an investment strategy where you invest a fixed amount of money at regular intervals, such as monthly or at every payday, regardless of market conditions.

Why It Works: By investing consistently, you buy more shares when prices are low and fewer when prices are high, reducing the risk of market volatility over time.

How to Apply It:
- Invest a set amount into your retirement accounts, such as an IRA or 401(k), each month.
- Use automated contributions to simplify the process and eliminate the temptation to time the market.

Tip: For example, contributing $200 every month to a broad index fund can generate significant growth over decades, even if the market has ups and do

2. Selecting Mutual Funds with Low Fees

Why Fees Matter: High fees can erode your investment returns over time. A mutual fund with a 1.5% annual fee may not sound high, but over 30 years, this can cost you thousands of dollars compared to a fund with a 0.1% fee.

What to Look For:
- Choose mutual funds with **low expense ratios** (ideally under 0.2%).

- Favor index funds, which often have lower fees compared to actively managed funds. What is an index fund? An index fund is a portfolio of stocks or bonds designed to mimic the composition and performance of a financial market index, such as the DOW or the S&P 500. Check for hidden fees, such as sales loads or administrative costs.
- While you are studying mutual funds, include in your homework assignment the ETF. The short definition is that an ETF is an exchange traded fund. There are some differences between an ETF and a Mutual Fund. An oversimplification would be that ETFs are more flexible, with intra-day trading, generally lower costs, and better tax efficiency. Mutual Funds are suitable for investors who prefer simplicity, no trading decisions, and automatic investments.
- Use tools like Morningstar or your brokerage firm to study which funds might be best for you.
- Consider your ethics and values. You might not want to look at index funds because of your personal values. Do you want to invest in the military? Do you want to look for a mutual fund that places emphasis on environmental issues? Do you want to avoid investing in companies that produce tobacco products or alcohol?

How to Apply It:

- Look for reputable low-cost funds such as Vanguard, Fidelity, or Schwab index funds.
- Use tools like Morningstar or your brokerage account to compare fund fees.

3. The Value of Emergency Funds

What It Is: An emergency fund is a savings cushion designed to cover 3 to 6 months of essential expenses in case of unexpected events like job loss, medical emergencies, or car repairs.

Why It Matters: Without an emergency fund, people often rely on high-interest debt (e.g., credit cards), which can create a financial snowball effect.

How to Build One:
- Start small: Aim for $500 to $1,000 as an initial goal. Once such an account is opened, work toward 3 to 6 months of living expenses.
- Use a high-yield savings account to keep this money accessible while earning some interest.
- Prioritize consistency: Save a small percentage of every paycheck until your fund is complete.

Tip: Automate monthly transfers into a designated emergency fund account to ensure steady progress.

4. Automating Savings and Investments

Why It Works: Automation removes human error and emotional decision-making from saving and investing. It ensures you "pay yourself first" and builds wealth effortlessly over time.

How to Apply It:
- Set up automatic transfers to savings accounts, investment accounts, and retirement funds.
- Contribute a percentage of each paycheck to a 401(k) or IRA automatically.
- Use tools like Acorns or your bank's automatic savings feature to round up purchases and save small amounts consistently.

5. Understanding and Avoiding High-Interest Debt

Why It Matters: This is one area that both Scripture and Secular agree. In earlier chapters, you have read the biblical wisdom about avoiding debt. Secular advisors will point out how high-interest debt, such as credit card balances, can quickly become unmanageable and derail your financial goals.

How to Avoid It:
- Pay off credit card balances in full each month to avoid interest charges.
- Use the **debt snowball** method (paying off the smallest debts first) or the **debt avalanche** method (paying off the highest-interest debts first) to eliminate existing debt.
- Build a strong emergency fund to prevent reliance on credit cards for unexpected expenses.

6. Investing in Tax-Advantaged Accounts

What They Are: Tax-advantaged accounts, such as 401(k)s, 403(b)s, IRAs, and HSAs, allow you to grow your money while minimizing taxes. Wait – what are these terms and what do they mean? Those mutual funds and ETFs we've mentioned earlier can be have tax advantages, or not. The 401(k), IRAs, and the rest of this list have tax advantages. This is part of your homework. They are not complicated. You can talk to your financial advisor about what is right for you.

Why They Matter: Over time, tax savings can dramatically boost your wealth.

How to Apply It:
- Contribute enough to your 401(k) or 403(b), to receive your employer's full match—this is free money. Not every employer will offer this, but if it is offered, take it.
- Maximize annual contributions to IRAs.

- Use Health Savings Accounts (HSAs) to save for medical expenses with triple tax advantages.

7. Diversification: Don't Put All Your Eggs in One Basket
What It Means: Diversification involves spreading your investments across different asset classes (stocks, bonds, real estate, etc.) to reduce risk.
How to Diversify:
- Invest in low-cost index funds that provide exposure to a broad range of assets.
- Allocate investments based on your age, goals, and risk tolerance (e.g., 60% stocks, 30% bonds, 10% alternatives).
- Consider international funds for additional diversification.

Tip: If you're unsure where to start, target-date funds automatically adjust your investment mix as you approach retirement.

8. Living Below Your Means
Why It's Key: Building wealth requires spending less than you earn. Simple habits like budgeting, avoiding lifestyle inflation, and cutting unnecessary expenses can have a massive impact over time.
How to Apply It:
- Track your spending with apps like Mint or YNAB (You Need a Budget).
- Save windfalls (e.g., bonuses, tax refunds) rather than spending them.
- Prioritize needs over wants and delay gratification to achieve long-term goals.

9. Selecting a Financial Advisor

One important bit of homework for you to do is to select a financial advisor. How do you do this?

First: Look for an Advisor Who Is a Fiduciary. A fiduciary is an individual who is ethically bound to act in another person's best interest. Fiduciary financial advisors must avoid conflicts of interest and disclose any potential conflicts of interest to clients.

Second: Meet and Interview More than One Advisor. You would not buy the first car you see on the lot. Nor would a person look at only one house to buy. This is a decision that takes time. Meet with a handful of advisors and prayerfully consider who is best for you and your family.

Third: Ask About Experience. I've had a few parishioners who became financial advisors with little training and no experience. Many of my parishioners were such people and I knew them to be fine, intelligent people. But I also knew they needed experience. I remember watching an old episode of the medical drama, St Elsewhere. The heart surgeon and his patient were talking about an upcoming heart transplant. "I guess you've done a lot of these," the patient said. "Nope," the doctor replied. "This is my first. I'm really looking forward to it." Even if the doctor had said, "I've assisted in several," the patient would have been more at ease.

Fourth: Ask About Credentials. To give investment advice, financial advisors must pass a test. Ask your advisor about their licenses, tests, and credentials. There are a lot of credentials an advisor might secure, such as a Certified

Financial Planner, or CFP. Ask each person you meet with what credentials he or she has and do some homework about what those particular credentials mean.

Fifth: Understand How They are Paid. Some advisors are "fee only" and charge you a flat rate. Some advisors charge a percentage of your assets under their management. Some advisors are paid commissions by mutual funds, which is a serious conflict of interest (why would I suggest a great mutual fund that pays me a low commission, when I could make a high commission selling you a fair or even poor performing mutual fund).

Sixth: **Will this Advisor Know You as an Individual.** My first financial advisor was a member of my Kiwanis Club, and we got to know each other. My second one didn't know me from Adam. We had a short relationship. The one I am with now is someone I've worked with for over 15 years. He knows that my wife and I are thrifty and are careful with our spending. He understands that I have a higher risk tolerance than might be advisable for a person my age, and that my wife has always been more conservative. He often brings this up in our conversation to be sure we are all on the same wavelength. It is not necessary for the advisor to know your favorite movies, but it is helpful for the advisor to know your financial needs and philosophy.

Final Thoughts: Faith, Wisdom, and Practicality

The biblical principles of stewardship, discipline, and generosity form the foundation for sound financial management. However, when paired with modern, proven strategies, they create a powerful toolkit for financial success. Remember:

- Be diligent and consistent with your savings and investments.
- Avoid unnecessary debt and manage existing obligations wisely.
- Focus on long-term goals while living a life of purpose and generosity.

Whether guided by faith, wisdom, or practicality, the keys to financial security remain universal: **spend less than you earn, save consistently, invest wisely, and stay patient.** By applying these principles, you can honor your values while building a stable and prosperous future for yourself and your loved ones.

"Wealth gained hastily will dwindle, but whoever gathers little by little will increase it." – Proverbs 13:11

Questions for Thought

1. What is your next step? Were you expecting more? Well, surprise – this single question is everything. It's up to you.

Appendix: Glossary

We've tossed some terms that you may or may not understand, so let's take a look at a glossary of secular financial terms. This is not an exhaustive glossary, but it is a starting point for you.

403(b): A tax-advantaged retirement plan available to employees of public schools, non-profits, and certain tax-exempt organizations, similar to a 401(k). As a pastor, I invested in 403(b)s.

401(k): An employer-sponsored retirement savings plan that allows employees to contribute a portion of their pre-tax income, often with employer matching contributions.

Asset Class: A type of investment, such as stocks, bonds, or money-market funds.

Bear Market: A financial market in which stock prices are falling and investors are pessimistic. A bear market is defined as a 20% drop from recent highs in indices or stocks.

Benchmark: A point of reference against which an investment's performance is measured.

Bonds: Securities that represent a loan of the investors' money to a business or government. You generally earn less with bonds than with stocks, so why invest in bonds? Bonds are riskier, meaning you may lose money. Bonds are safer than stocks because the borrower has committed to return the principal. With stocks, investors may put $100 of equity into a company, but they may lose it all if the company goes bankrupt, but bondholders, by law, will be paid first and may get everything that the company has left.

Bull Market: A financial market in which stock prices are rising and investor sentiment is positive. How do you remember which is good and which is not so good when talking about bear markets and bull markets. Keep in mind the statue of the bull on Wall Street – no one celebrates the bear, so the bull is better.

Capital Gains: Your capital gain (or loss) is the difference between the sale price of your investment and the cost basis. **The "cost basis"** is a term used in United States tax law, and it is the original cost of property, adjusted for factors such as depreciation.

CD, or Certificate of Deposit: A certificate of deposit (CD) is a type of savings account that pays a fixed interest rate on money held for an agreed-upon period of time, such as a few months or evey a few years. The best CD rates are usually higher than savings accounts, but you lose withdrawal flexibility. If you withdraw early, you pay a penalty.

Commodities: Basic goods used in commerce, like oil, wheat, or gold.

Common Stock: Shares of ownership in a business.

Diversification: Spreading investments across different assets to reduce risk.

Dividend: A payment made by a company to its shareholders, usually a portion of its profits, typically distributed quarterly. Not every stock pays dividends. Their value is when you sell the stock at a profit (hopefully instead of a loss).

Exchange-Traded Fund: An investment fund that is also traded on the stock exchange.

Expense Ratio: The ratio of a fund's operating expenses to its total assets, showing how much is being spent on administrative costs.

Futures: Contracts that agree to buy or sell an asset at a specific price on a certain date in the future. This is not an important term for beginners, but you may hear about it in the news or in movies.

Hedge Fund: A fund that invests in a variety of asset types and employs creative strategies, often including higher risk, to earn higher returns. There are usually very high minimums, making it beyond the reach of a beginning investor, which is good for you. You probably don't need the higher risk.

HSA (Health Savings Account): A tax-advantaged savings account for individuals with high-deductible health plans (HDHPs), allowing tax-free contributions, growth, and withdrawals for qualified medical expenses.

Index Fund: A mutual fund that invests in a way that tracks a certain market index, often the S&P 500.

Interest: The cost of borrowing money or the return earned on savings or investments, typically expressed as a percentage.

IPO: Initial public offering, the first offering of a company's stock for sale to the public.

IRA (Individual Retirement Account): A tax-advantaged account that allows individuals to save for retirement with either pre-tax or post-tax contributions. **Roth IRA:** A type of IRA where contributions are made with after-tax income, and withdrawals, including earnings, are tax-free in retirement if certain conditions are met.

Limit Order: An order to buy or sell an asset when its value hits a specific price.

Margin Trading: Borrowing money to buy stocks, using the shares themselves as collateral. This is probably something you will participate in, but it is a term you may hear on the news or in movies.
Market Order: An order to buy or sell an asset immediately, regardless of its current price.

Money Market Fund: A mutual fund that invests in short-term debts with low risk.

Mutual Fund: A pool of money invested in a variety of assets, such as stocks. Investing in individual stocks offers risk, requires time to research, and lacks diversification. Investing in a mutual fund means you are investing in many companies and there are fund managers taking care of the fund. It is often considered safer and simpler than investing in individual stocks.

No-Load Fund: A fund that doesn't charge a commission for buying or selling shares. This is a good term to look for when looking for a mutual fund in which to invest.

P/E Ratio: This is a way to value a company by comparing the price of a stock to its earnings. The P/E equals the price of a share of stock, divided by the company's earnings-per-share. It tells you how much you are paying for each dollar of earnings.

Preferred Stock: A type of stock that gives priority to its holders when dividends are distributed.

Prospectus: A document describing a specific security for potential investors. They are not fun and entertaining to read, but they do provide useful information.

Short Selling: A process by which an investor borrows shares of stock and sells them, waits for the share price to fall, then buys the shares back and returns them to the lender. Ultimately, the investor profits from the stock's loss of value, while the original owner of the shares makes money by charging a borrowing fee to the investor. This is not a concern for a beginner in investing.

Stop-Loss Order: An order to sell an asset at a certain price in order to limit the investor's losses.

Treasury Bond: A bond representing long-term government debt.

Volatility: The amount of variation in the price of an asset over time.

Yield: The annualized amount shown as a percentage an investor earns in interest or dividends from an investment.

www.ingramcontent.com/pod-product-compliance
Lightning Source LLC
Chambersburg PA
CBHW050301230526
45471CB00005B/1969